120+ ghost towns, natural wonders, and other off-the-beaten-path destinations

Hidden Newfoundland

Scott Osmond

BOULDER
BOOKS

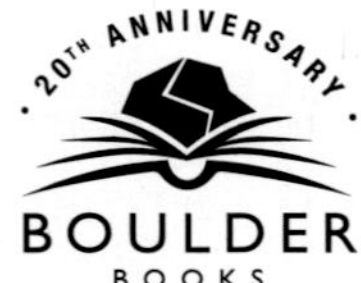

Library and Archives Canada Cataloguing in Publication

Title: Hidden Newfoundland : 120+ ghost towns, natural wonders,
and other off-the-beaten path destinations / Scott Osmond.
Names: Osmond, Scott, author.
Description: Includes bibliographical references and index.
Identifiers: Canadiana 20210283688 | ISBN 9781989417324 (softcover)
Subjects: LCSH: Newfoundland and Labrador—Description and travel. | LCSH:
Newfoundland and Labrador—
   Guidebooks. | LCSH: Ghost towns—Newfoundland and Labrador. | LCSH:
Curiosities and wonders—
   Newfoundland and Labrador. | LCSH: Newfoundland and Labrador—Miscellanea.
Classification: LCC FC2167.6 .O86 2021 | DDC 917.1804/5—dc23

Published by Boulder Books

Portugal Cove-St. Philip's, Newfoundland and Labrador
www.boulderbooks.ca

Design and layout: Tanya Montini
Editor: Stephanie Porter
Copy editor: Iona Bulgin

Printed in China

We acknowledge the financial support of the Government of Newfoundland and
Labrador through the Department of Tourism, Culture, Arts and Recreation.

Funded by the Government of Canada
Financé par le gouvernement du Canada

Canada

*I dedicate this book to the friends and family
who have helped and supported me along the way.*

*But most of all, I dedicate it to my partner
and adventure companion, who never says no
to adventure, and whose relentless and unwavering
support truly made this book possible.
Lindsay, this book is for you.*

Table of Contents

KATHLEEN II

THE GREAT NORTHERN PENINSULA
1. CHIMNEY COVE
2. LOMOND AND STANLEYVILLE
3. PISSING MARE FALLS
4. MIDDLE BROOK FALLS & SWIMMING HOLE
5. THE OLD MAN
6. COW HEAD LIGHTHOUSE
7. ST. ANTHONY RADAR STATION
8. SS *EMPIRE ENERGY*
9. BIG BROOK
10. HAND-BUILT SHIPS OF BIDE ARM
11. THE UNDERGROUND SALMON RIVER
12. CONCHE HARBOUR LIGHTHOUSE
13. CONCHE PLANE CRASH
14. GLASS HOLE
15. LOST AIRSTRIPS OF THE NORTHERN PENINSULA

WEST COAST
1. GRAND LAKE
2. MAIN DAM
3. SERPENTINE VALLEY
4. LOMOND SINKHOLE
5. SINKHOLES & DISAPPEARING STREAMS
6. CORNER BROOK STREAM CAVES
7. VALMONT DRIVE-IN
8. YORK HARBOUR MINE
9. CEDAR COVE
10. GOVERNOR'S STAIRCASE
11. BOTTLE COVE SEA CAVE
12. COPPER MINE FALLS
13. SWIMMING HOLE ATOP STEADY BROOK FALLS
14. CORNER BROOK QUARRY FALLS

SOUTHWEST COAST
1. EARNEST HARMON AIR FORCE BASE
2. BLANCHE BROOK
3. GYPSUM CLIFFS & A SINKHOLE FOREST
4. WESTERN PINETREE LINE RADAR STATION
5. FOX ISLAND LIGHTHOUSE
6. THE GRAVELS WALKING TRAIL
7. LEAD COVE MINE
8. AGUATHUNA LIMESTONE QUARRY
9. WEST BAY & JERRY'S NOSE TRANSMITTER SITES
10. KISSING ROCKS SEA ARCH
11. LONG POINT
12. PORT AU PORT CRASH
13. HIGHLANDS SEA STACKS
14. RED ROCKS BUILDING
15. MV *SADIE AND EVA*

CENTRAL NEWFOUNDLAND
1. THE TOPSAILS
2. BUCHANS MINE
3. THUNDER BROOK FALLS
4. BOTWOOD'S SEAPLANE BASE
5. PHILLIPS HEAD & WISEMANS HEAD BATTERY
6. FJORDS OF THE SOUTH COAST
7. GREY RIVER TUNGSTEN MINE

EAST COAST
1. DUNGEON PROVINCIAL PARK
2. BONAVISTA AIRSTRIP
3. ARCH ROCK
4. TOWN OF PORT UNION
5. THE TRINITY LOOP
6. TERRA NOVA SULPHITE COMPANY PULP MILL
7. BURGOYNES COVE B-36 CRASH
8. BLACK BROOK FALLS
9. NEWFOUNDLAND'S FIRST PULP MILL
10. THE WRECK OF *SENATOR PENNY*
11. ST. LAWRENCE FLUORSPAR MINES
12. CHAMBERS COVE

WHITE BAY TO GREEN BAY
1. SOP'S ARM BARGE
2. CONEY ARM & EASTERN BROOK FALLS
3. CAT ARM HYDRO FACILITY & CONSTRUCTION TUNNELS
4. RATTLE BROOK SPILLWAY
5. TILT COVE COPPER MINE
6. BAIE VERTE ASBESTOS MINE
7. KING'S POINT RATTLING BROOK FALLS
8. GLASSY BEACH
9. PILLEY'S ISLAND MINE
10. LITTLE BAY ISLANDS

LEWISPORTE TO BONAVISTA BAY
1. HMS *CALYPSO/BRITON*
2. HORWOOD LUMBER COMPANY MILL
3. SS *AHERN TRADER SHIPWRECK*
4. SIR FREDERICK BANTING'S PLANE CRASH
5. SLEEPY COVE MINE
6. *MISS BAYVIEW II* AND SOUTH TWILLINGATE ISLAND FERRY TERMINAL
7. LOWER LITTLE HARBOUR SEA ARCH
8. GANDER AMMUNITION BUNKERS
9. THE "TURKEY FARM"
10. THOMAS HOWE DEMONSTRATION FOREST CRASH SITE

TRINITY BAY & CONCEPTION BAY WEST
1. SS *CHARCOT,* SS *SOUTHERN FOAM,* & SS *SUKHA*
2. HAMILTON BANKER
3. BRIGUS TUNNEL
4. SS *KYLE*
5. RIDLEY HALL
6. NORTH AMERICA'S FIRST CIVILIAN AIRPORT
7. THE OVERFALLS
8. NORTHERN BAY SEA ARCH
9. MOUSE HOLE ARCH
10. NEW HARBOUR TROUT FARM PROJECT
11. HOPEALL FALLS
12. CHANCE COVE COASTAL TRAIL
13. COLLIER POINT BARITE MINE

NORTHEAST AVALON
1. BELL ISLAND MINES
2. BELL ISLAND BATTERY
3. THE BELL
4. KELLIGREWS ABANDONED POOL
5. NASA'S SATELLITE TRACKING STATION
6. RED CLIFF RADAR STATION
7. CENTRAL SWINE BREEDING STATION
8. FORT AMHERST
9. CHAIN ROCK
10. BOWRING PARK CANTILEVER BRIDGE
11. BROOKFIELD DRIVE-IN
12. MILITARY BATTERIES OF THE EAST COAST

PLACENTIA BAY & THE SOUTHERN AVALON PENINSULA
1. LA MANCHE LEAD MINE
2. LA MANCHE COMMUNITY
3. SPENCER'S COVE
4. *FUMI MARU NO. 15* SHIPWRECK
5. ARGENTIA NAVAL AIR BASE & FORT MCANDREW
6. ISAAC HEAD BATTERY
7. ROCKY RIVER WATERFALL AND BRIDGE
8. CATARACTS PROVINCIAL PARK
9. BAY BULLS HYDROELECTRIC FACILITY
10. THE SPOUT
11. SS *ILEX*
12. LA MANCHE
13. SPOUT RIVER FALLS
14. BERRY HEAD SEA ARCH

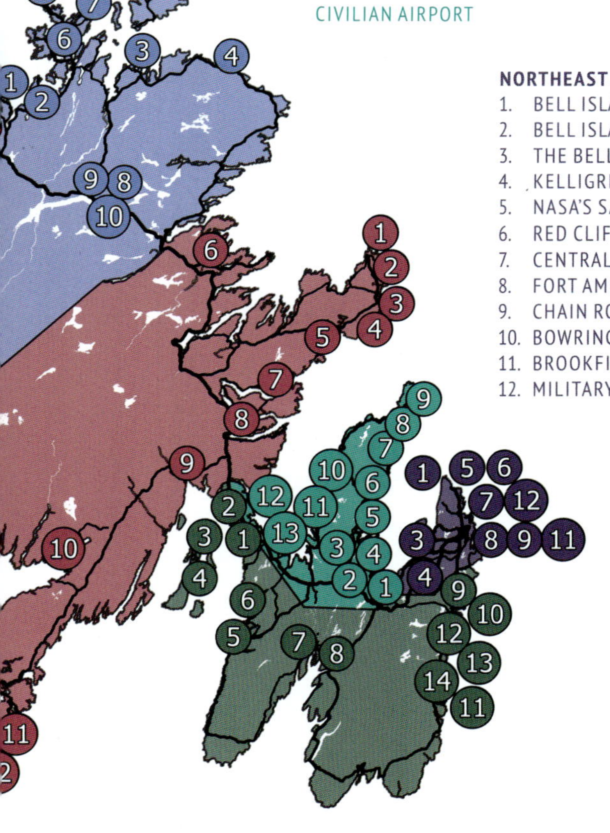

Introduction

About this Guide

Newfoundland and Labrador is known for its rich history, culture, and scenery. Every year, thousands of tourists venture to the province to see the famous lighthouses of Bonavista and Cape Spear, the icebergs that pass by St. Anthony and Twillingate, and the fjords of the Long Range Mountains in Gros Morne National Park.

I would never dissuade anyone from visiting these destinations, but Newfoundland and Labrador has so much more to offer than what is found within the confines of an average tourism guide.

This province is filled with geologic wonders, mysterious histories, curious structures, and off-the-beaten-path destinations. From unexplored cave systems to the remains of Cold War-era aircraft, deteriorating churches in long resettled communities to abandoned air force bases, the remains of an early pulp mill to intricate underground mines, this book will take you to many unusual and peculiar locations around Newfoundland and Labrador.

This guide is for explorers—novice and experienced, local and come-from-away—who wish to see more of Newfoundland and experience places that have been lost, forgotten, or are yet-to-be-found.

I hope to do three things in this guide:

Introduce new places to visit and explore

The selection of destinations in this guide has not been influenced by ease of access, politics, or economic value. Just because a place does not meet the economic or political viability of many tourism sites does not mean it is not worth sharing. In many cases, these places outshine more popular destinations.

Promote Newfoundland's incredible built and natural heritage

Each location represents a piece of Newfoundland and Labrador's history and development. I hope to raise awareness of cultural, historic, and geologic preservation while also sharing forgotten stories.

Show that exploring is for everyone

Whether you wish to explore the wonders of Newfoundland from a car or are looking for a new hiking destination, this guide is for you. And if you're an armchair explorer, I hope this book brings these places alive and inspires wonder for you, wherever you are.

USING THIS GUIDE

Assumption of Risk

Many of the places in this guide are abandoned and/or unmarked, and therefore risky to visit. This guide provides general information about each place, its history, and its location. Proper caution and safety must be taken at all times.

This guide does not encourage illegal, illicit, or dangerous activities. Those who visit the described locations do so at their own risk, and proper safety precautions must be taken.

Here are some basic reminders to ensure a safe adventure:

- Know before you go. Research and understand potential risks.
- Use extra caution around edges, cliffs, steep hillsides, and the ocean.
- Never enter an unmaintained or abandoned building/structure due to risk of falling debris, collapse, and other hidden dangers. Obtain permission to enter any structures or private properties.
- Take out what you take in and leave the area as it was when you arrived.

It is the sole responsibility of the explorer to determine whether it is safe to explore or visit any of the places listed here.

LAND ACKNOWLEDGEMENT

Before we begin exploring, we must respectfully acknowledge that the island of Newfoundland and the territory in which we are travelling is the ancestral homeland of the Beothuk and Mi'kmaq. Although this guide focuses on the island portion of the province, I would also like to recognize the Inuit of Nunatsiavut and NunatuKavut and the Innu of Nitassinan, and their ancestors, as the original people of Labrador.

The Origin of Newfoundland's Lost Wonders

The obscure places discussed in this book are not only scattered across the province but also varied in how they were produced.

NATURAL WONDERS & CURIOUS LANDSCAPES

The story of how Newfoundland came to be is filled with tales of continents colliding and then being torn apart, forming new oceans before repeating the process. On the east coast of the island of Newfoundland and on the Avalon Peninsula, 500- to 700-million-year-old rocks have preserved important evolutions of life on Earth, including the earliest record of large, complex multicellular life (Mistaken Point) and the oldest-known complex muscled organism (Discovery Global Geopark).

Between 500 and 430 million years ago, one of the most significant geologic events to shape the island of Newfoundland occurred: the opening of the Iapetus Ocean, the predecessor to the Atlantic Ocean. During this period, sediment accumulation formed the sedimentary and carbonate rocks that comprise much of the west and central areas of the island along the edges of the vast ocean. Volcanic activity continued to produce new rocks.

As the Iapetus Ocean closed and its water evaporated, a large dried-up basin similar to that of California's Death Valley was formed. This was a turbulent time: plate tectonics began closing the ocean and, concurrently, the Appalachian Mountains formed, thrusting large chunks of ocean floor upward, producing the ophiolite complexes that now make up Newfoundland's highest mountains of Lewis Hills, Blow Me Down Mountains, and the Tablelands. These exposed pieces of the Earth's deepest solid

layers can be seen only in a few places around the world.

The Quaternary period of Earth's story represents the period between 2.58 million years ago and today. During this time, the Earth went through a major ice age. Extensive glaciers covered Newfoundland; as they moved across the land, they carved islands, fjords, valleys, and a rocky, barren landscape. As the glaciers melted, new lakes and rivers formed, which carved new valleys and deposited vast amounts of sand, silt, and gravel across the island. Everything from smooth, rocky landscapes to caves and sinkholes were created by these giants.

THE INDUSTRIES THAT SHAPED THE LAND

Newfoundlanders have struggled for over 500 years to create sustainable livelihoods. In the early days of the seasonal European fishery, harsh weather and poor seafaring conditions limited those who could survive. But many did. And as the population of the island grew, so did the demand for new industries. The result: almost every small community of Newfoundland has a remnant of an industry that either once provided its livelihood or promised work that never came. What is left provides opportunities to learn about Newfoundland's heritage.

Mining in Newfoundland

Some of the first people to use the products of Newfoundland's geology were the Dorset Paleo-Eskimos, who used soapstone from cliffs near Fleur de Lys to carve bowls and tools. Starting with European colonization nearly 1,000 years later, mining operations became more complex. Since the 18th century, thousands of mines have been excavated. While in many cases these operations brought just a few years of work, others resulted in enormous operations that stretched for nearly a century. No industry in Newfoundland has left behind more relicts and places to explore.

Forestry & logging

At the end of the 19th century, the newly constructed Newfoundland Railway provided new access to the island's interior, igniting a fury of pulp, paper, and sawmills. Small family-owned sawmills gave rise to massive pulp and paper industries that led to the construction of the Grand Falls and Corner Brook pulp and paper mills. Some of these mills operate successfully in 2021, but in many cases, project viability, lack of resources, and financial insecurity forced closure.

The Newfoundland Railway

The Newfoundland Railway has long been a source of pride and a symbol of nationalism for the people of Newfoundland. Its construction began in 1881 in St. John's. After a bumpy start, a line was constructed from the province's capital to the ferry terminal in Channel-Port aux Basques, with many branch lines connecting such towns as Bonavista, Carbonear, and Placentia. The railway ran through the mostly uninhabited interior of Newfoundland and was key in opening up this area to industry. After the construction of the Trans-Canada Highway in 1965, the need for a railway diminished, and in 1969 passenger service ceased, followed by the last freight transport in 1988.

Diversifying economies

Newfoundland was built around the fishery. But the industry was never large enough to "modernize" Newfoundland the way so many wanted. While many politicians and businesspeople attempted to diversify the province's economy, no one tried harder than Newfoundland and Labrador's first premier, Joey Smallwood. Throughout the second half of the 20th century, the Smallwood government marketed Newfoundland around the world. This resulted in plants and factories that produced everything from cement and gypsum to rubber boots and chocolate bars. But good marketing and incentives only go so far, and as quickly as many of these businesses appeared, they disappeared. Some managed to continue operation for upward of 50 and 60 years, such as Atlantic Gypsum in Corner Brook, but most did not. The remains of this period in the province's economic history can be found throughout the island.

THE STORY OF RESETTLEMENT

Smallwood and his governments were also responsible for the controversial resettlement programs of the 1950s, 1960s, and 1970s. Newfoundland had been no stranger to resettlement before Smallwood—it would not be a stretch to say that every place a boat could be pulled ashore and a house built, it was. Many of the island's thousands of protected coves, harbours, and inlets contained a small community whose only connection to the outside was by boat. Coastal boat services, such as the Reid Family's Alphabet Fleet, regularly brought supplies and trading opportunities to these towns. This sparsely populated system was unsustainable, and as more connected communities grew, others naturally diminished.

In 1954, Smallwood introduced the Centralization Program, which was the first phase of a resettlement program that offered residents of small, unconnected communities financial incentives to move to more established towns. At first, community residents had to unanimously agree to relocate to receive the benefits. Between the start of the program in 1954 and 1965, 7,500 people from 110 communities resettled. The second phase of resettlement came in 1965 and was assisted by the federal government. This new program dictated that only 90 per cent of a community's residents had to agree to leave (later changed to 80 per cent), and between 1965 and 1974, nearly 20,000 people from 148 communities agreed to accept the government's money and relocate.

The relocation programs were met with mixed emotions. Many people were thankful for the opportunity to move to places where more work and education opportunities existed; but the move came with the heavy price of losing homes, livelihoods, and culture. Newfoundland resettlement continues to this day.

For the very reasons these communities were resettled, many are difficult to visit. Most are now nothing more than empty fields with the occasional house. Others have been transformed into bustling cabin communities. Each resettled community has its own charm to be discovered, whether that be physical remnants or magnificent scenery or both.

Militarization of an unexpected nation

Stretching back almost 500 years, Newfoundland and Labrador's waters have been involved in English, French, Spanish, and Portuguese conflict. Rusted cannons and the remnants of military forts and barracks can be found in many coastal communities.

During the wars of the 20th century, the province's strategic location in the North Atlantic meant that it became the epicentre for military operations in the Atlantic Ocean. American, Canadian, and British forces all claimed land across the island to construct military bases, airfields, and radar stations. These locations were designed for everything from the delivery of military supplies to Europe during the world wars to tracking Soviet aircraft and missiles during the Cold War.

World War I dramatically affected the people and island of Newfoundland. But as far as physical evidence goes, World War II had a more visible impact. Newfoundland was the first line of defence for North America and a necessary refuelling location for aircraft and ships travelling to the war in Europe. Canadian and British outposts were established, including the seaplane base in Botwood. Protective defences were built along the east coast to protect supply ships travelling from North America to Europe.

British prime minister Winston Churchill knew that Britain needed warships to defeat Germany in the North Atlantic. Meanwhile, the US began worrying about Germany invading North America if the UK was defeated. The solution to both countries' problems came on September 2, 1940, when US

and UK leaders met in Ship Cove, Newfoundland, to make the Destroyers for Bases Agreement. In exchange for 50 aging destroyer warships, the US was granted 99-year British land leases on the island of Newfoundland. This sparked an era of militarization, with dozens of military bases, defence bunkers, and radar stations being built across Newfoundland.

Not long afterWorld War II ended, the Cold War began. Many of the province's air force bases and naval stations were upgraded and new radar sites were constructed to detect Soviet aircraft and missiles flying over the Arctic and the Atlantic Ocean. As tensions between the US and Soviet Union eased and new technology was developed, the need for Newfoundland as a military site diminished.

The use of the island by these foreign powers has been dubbed the "Friendly Invasion." Stephenville, Gander, and Botwood were all built around, and benefited from, the construction of these military bases. The remains of military buildings and concrete foundations are scattered across Newfoundland's landscape.

BY LAND AND SEA

Sailing & shipping

Newfoundlanders' determination to live near, travel by, and make a living from the sea is second to none. But the island's location in the north Atlantic Ocean and its rocky, jagged coastline has meant that disaster is never far away. Dotting the coast of the island are thousands of shipwrecks. While the sea has pulled many of these out of sight, many more pierce the surface, offering a reminder of how unforgiving the ocean can be.

Aviation history

Throughout the early years of aviation, Newfoundland's location as the easternmost point in North America made it critical for pilots looking to make the perilous transatlantic crossing. In 1919, John Alcock and Arthur Brown departed St. John's and made the first non-stop flight across the Atlantic Ocean. Soon afterwards, North America's first airport was established in the town of Harbour Grace. Pilots from around the world began taking off from Harbour Grace, helping lead to the revolution of long-distance air travel. One such pilot was Amelia Earhart, who became the first female pilot to fly solo across the Atlantic Ocean after leaving Harbour Grace. In the late 1930s a seaplane base in Botwood and an international airport in Gander were established, aimed specifically at refuelling aircraft travelling from Europe to North America. Through the Second World War, air force bases were established, and Gander International Airport became known as the "crossroads of the world."

While advances in aviation and technology made the need for Newfoundland as a stopover point obsolete, airports in Gander,

St. John's, and Stephenville continue to welcome enormous cargo planes and military aircraft.

The remnants of aviation disasters can also be seen across the province. These fragments of the province's sombre heritage are memorials to those who were lost.

Many aircraft crash sites on the island today are protected under the Historic Resources Act which prohibits the removal of any artifacts. When visiting, please be respectful and leave each place as you find it.

Exploring Newfoundland Safely

CLIMATE

The most dangerous and unpredictable hazard that will be encountered in Newfoundland is the weather.

The province's location provides it with a temperate, marine climate. The climate is cooler in Newfoundland than in Labrador, with an overall average daily temperature of 16°C (61°F) in the summer and 0°C (32°F) in the winter. The south-travelling Labrador Current delivers cold Arctic air and water to the eastern side of the Northern Peninsula and north coast of the island, while the Gulf Stream from the south provides a wet and mild climate to the south coast. These two opposing currents mix off the east coast of the Avalon Peninsula, causing the rain, drizzle, and fog that the area is known for. The west coast and central parts of the island are typically warmer than the rest of the province in the summer but experience cooler temperatures and higher snowfall amounts during the winter.

The best advice for anyone travelling the province is never to trust the forecast and prepare for everything!

HUNTING SEASON

The big-game hunting season in Newfoundland stretches through the fall and into early winter. If you are hiking or exploring Newfoundland's backcountry, make sure you are visible. Wear blaze orange or bright yellow so you are easy to identify. Make sure your pets are visible as well.

Check with the Newfoundland and Labrador Department of Wildlife website to see what hunting seasons are open and where.

ENVIRONMENTAL CONDITIONS

Heights & loose rocks

Many hiking trails and lookouts will bring you into the vicinity of cliffs or other steep slopes. Always wear proper footwear, maintain a safe distance from the edge, and use extra caution when deteriorating weather or water has caused slippery conditions.

Avoid going too close to rock cuts and cliffs, as falling rock can be extremely dangerous. Look for fractured rocks and areas that look more prone to collapse.

Ocean hazards

Never turn your back on the ocean. Keep a close eye on waves, tides, and changing weather conditions. Slippery rocks and quickly changing sea conditions can pose extreme hazards.

Abandoned buildings & deteriorated structures

Do not to enter any of the neglected, deteriorated, or abandoned buildings and structures described in this book. In addition to concerns about falling debris, collapsing structures, and mould or other airborne bacteria or chemicals, many places remain under private or government ownership and exploring them can be considered trespassing.

Almost all the places described in this book can and should be experienced from a safe distance. With some preparation and foresight, they can still be exciting and safe places to visit.

Cook's Harbour
9 8
Eddies Cove
Flower's Cove
Main Brook
15
7
Plum Point
11
Conche
12 13
10
14
Port au Choix
Englee
Hawke's Bay
La Scie
Portland Creek
Baie Verte
Parson's Pond
Cow Head
6
3
Rocky Harbour
Trout River
Hampden
Springdale
5
2
1
4
Deer Lake
Corner Brook

The Great Northern Peninsula

Gros Morne National Park & the Great Northern Peninsula

The Great Northern Peninsula is nearly 200 kilometres long and 85 kilometres wide, stretching from Gros Morne National Park to the northern tip of the island of Newfoundland. In the south, Gros Morne National Park hosts some of the best views of the towering Long Range Mountains. Farther north, the mountains shift inland and the coastal terrace tells the story of thousands of years of human history. Travelling northward, it is easy to forgive the harsh climate as you witness thousands of whales and towering icebergs that call the region home each summer. The area offers some of the best of Newfoundland but only to those willing to go out of their way to enjoy it.

The history of the Great Northern Peninsula begins with the settlement of the Maritime Archaic people near Port aux Choix between 3,300 and 4,400 years ago. These first people eventually left and were replaced by the Groswater Paleo-Eskimos, the Dorset Paleo-Eskimos, and finally the Beothuk and Mi'kmaq in the southern portions of the peninsula. The Great Northern Peninsula was also the site of the first European explorers to arrive in North America, the Vikings. These Norse seafarers are believed to have only settled for a short period. It was not until the 16th century that Europeans, mainly from England and France, began settling along the coast.

Permanent settlement in the region did not occur until later in the 18th and 19th centuries. Beginning in the 19th and early 20th century, the onshore and Labrador fisheries provided livelihoods to those living in the scattered coastal communities and settlements. For many years the only way to travel between communities was by boat, until later in the 20th century when road networks were finally constructed through the area. The peninsula's proximity to Labrador helped towns such as St. Anthony become the gateway to Labrador and the north. In 1973, Gros Morne National Park was established, recognizing and preserving the majestic scenery, landscape, and geology. After the collapse of the cod fishery in 1992, tourism has become the main lifeline for many communities throughout the Great Northern Peninsula.

Leaving Deer Lake, the Viking Trail (Route 430) is the main highway "down" (as locals say) the coast. The highway runs 420 kilometres before ending in St. Anthony. In the south, Route 431 branches off near Wiltondale and offers some of the best of Gros Morne, leading to the beautiful communities of Woody Point and Trout River and providing a close-up look at the otherworldly Tablelands. In the north near St. Anthony, several small highways connect the communities of Raleigh, Cook's Harbour, and Saint Lunaire-Griquet. Be sure to complete the Route 432 loop, which provides access to the roads leading to Englee, Roddickton, and Conche before continuing and rejoining the Viking Trail (Route 430) in the community of Plum Point.

1. Chimney Cove

Trout River

Chimney Cove is a small picturesque resettled community located on the banks of the Gregory River on Newfoundland's west coast. While most of the houses that once made up the community no longer exist, cabins, fishing boats, and visitors from nearby Trout River keep this community alive 50 years after abandonment.

The community sits in a flat river valley. Small farms were constructed by settlers, and the surrounding forest was logged—but the community's main source of income was fishing because of its proximity to lobster fishing grounds. While the first record of settlers in Chimney Cove occurred in the late 1870s, the first census was not completed until 1884, which showed 100 people living there, most employed in the lobster fishery. By the end of the 1800s, Chimney Cove was one of the highest-yielding lobster settlements on the west coast.

The fishing industry continued to increase into the early 20th century. Family-run lobster factories drove the economy, with five factories in operation by 1911. Herring fishing was also a thriving industry by the 1920s.

In the 1930s and 1940s, many residents began using the area for agriculture. After the 1950s, the community's population began to steadily decrease. After several nearby communities were abandoned, Chimney Cove's remoteness and lack of amenities led many residents to leave. By 1968, all of Chimney Cove's residents and families had resettled, many to the nearby community of Trout River.

This community is a hidden gem tucked away in the mountains of the west coast. The flat river valley where the community once was and adjacent mountains make this one of the prettiest places to visit on the west coast.

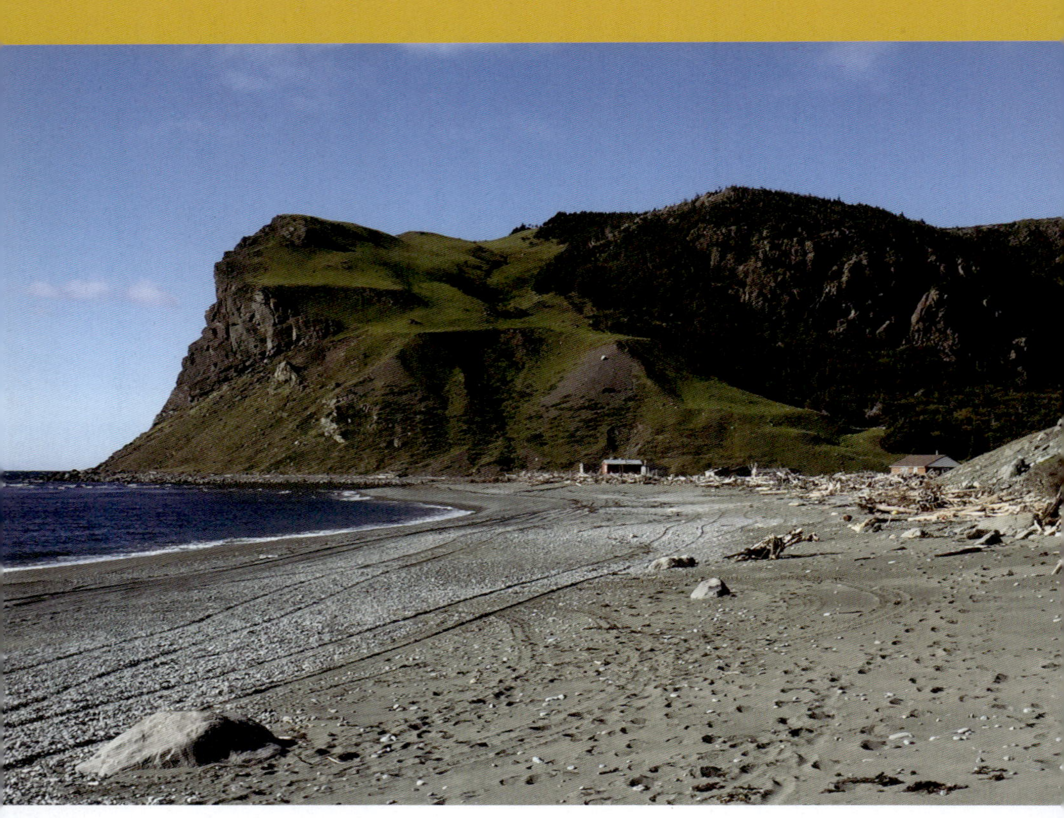

The easiest way to access Chimney Cove is by snowmobile or ATV. It may be possible to get there in an off-road vehicle; however, the road and river crossing can be unpredictable. Hiking is also an option but may require an overnight stay in the community.

The route to Chimney Cove is a gravel road located at the start of Trout River Pond (N 49.460636, W 58.119929). Travel on the road until you reach the Trout River Campground approximately 1.8 kilometres in. From there, the road slowly deteriorates. Travel 11.4 kilometres (staying right at the few notable intersections) and you will arrive at Gregory River. Follow the trail for about 550 metres and cross the river to arrive at the community.

2. Lomond and Stanleyville

East Arm, Bonne Bay

Situated in the beautiful East Arm of Bonne Bay are the abandoned communities of Stanleyville and Lomond. Both communities emerged during the logging revolution that occurred in Newfoundland around the end of the 19th century.

No permanent residents remain in either community. Lomond has become a popular camping and day park in Gros Morne National Park. As for Stanleyville, the only remnants of this once-thriving community are pieces of equipment and machinery that were once used in the town's sawmill. However, Stanleyville is one of the most picturesque coves in Newfoundland.

STANLEYVILLE

Once known as Paynes Cove, the community of Stanleyville began to grow when John and Scobie McKie from Nova Scotia set up a steam-powered sawmill in the small cove in the early 1890s. While many locals had come to call the cove Billy McKie's or Billy McKitt's cove, by the turn of the century the community was officially named Stanleyville. With the sawmill operating, new jobs were created and more people began to settle there.

Forty-eight people lived in the town in 1901; the population grew to 77 by 1911. At the time, the sawmill was worth $3,000 and employed 13 people. The mill was always the largest employer in the town; a number of residents were also engaged in boatbuilding.

In 1916, the St. Lawrence Timber, Pulp, and Steamship Company bought the McKie sawmill along with its 10,360 hectares of timber rights. Stanleyville's isolated location prohibited any

further expansion of the mill and, two years later, in 1918, the new owners set up another, much larger mill nearby in Murphy's Cove (later renamed Lomond). That mill would soon become one of the largest in Newfoundland.

Several people remained in Stanleyville until the middle of the century, but over the next several decades the cove was completely abandoned.

LOMOND

A Nova Scotia firm set up a small sawmill in Murphy's Cove in the late 19th century for producing spars (sail rigging) for sailing ships. The cove did not see much growth until 1916 when the St. Lawrence Timber, Pulp, and Steamship Company moved their logging operations from Stanleyville. The company soon

began construction on a steam mill and a company town, which included a wharf, school, and houses.

The logging operation grew and so did the community. In 1921, Murphy's Cove was renamed Lomond and a census from the same year reports 88 permanent residents. By then, construction had begun on a much larger pulp and paper mill in Corner Brook. The community and mill eventually peaked in the 1940s when it was recorded that 400 people were working in the town and the timber being processed there was being exported to Canada and Europe.

The mill was taken over by Bowater Inc. in the 1940s. In the 1950s, the company shut the mill down, mainly due to the mill's viability compared to others nearby, and difficulties in accessing uncut forest.

After the mill was shut down, efforts were made to preserve the

local economy. In 1960, a $17,000 fishway was constructed to help replenish the Lomond River's overfished salmon population. The government had hoped that by restoring the salmon stocks it could one day be used again for sportfishing and attract local fishers.

In 1973, Gros Morne National Park was established, forcing the relocation of the remaining 14 families in Lomond. The former woods manager's residence was converted to a sportfishing lodge. The lodge and surrounding land were later acquired by the Church of England to be used for retreats and continue to operate as a popular summer camp named Killdevil.

ABOUT THE AREA

Today Lomond has been transformed into a campground and day park. The surrounding views of the Long Range Mountains, in particular Killdevil Mountain, have made the park one of the top spots to visit and camp in Gros Morne. At the far side of the park, the remnants of the mill are still visible throughout the forest. Tall concrete walls and building foundations continue to serve as a historic reminder of the logging town.

From the far side of the park, a short but difficult hiking trail crawls over a steep hill before bringing you to the quaint cove of Stanleyville. Here among the wetlands behind a rocky beach, rusting pieces of equipment appear in distinctive contrast to the lush green forest behind it. Not all evidence of the community has been lost to time, however; nearby in Killdevil Camp, the woods manager's residence is still used by camp employees in 2021.

Little may be left of the town and mills, but the area still has many relics of past industry, as well as stunning panoramic landscapes.

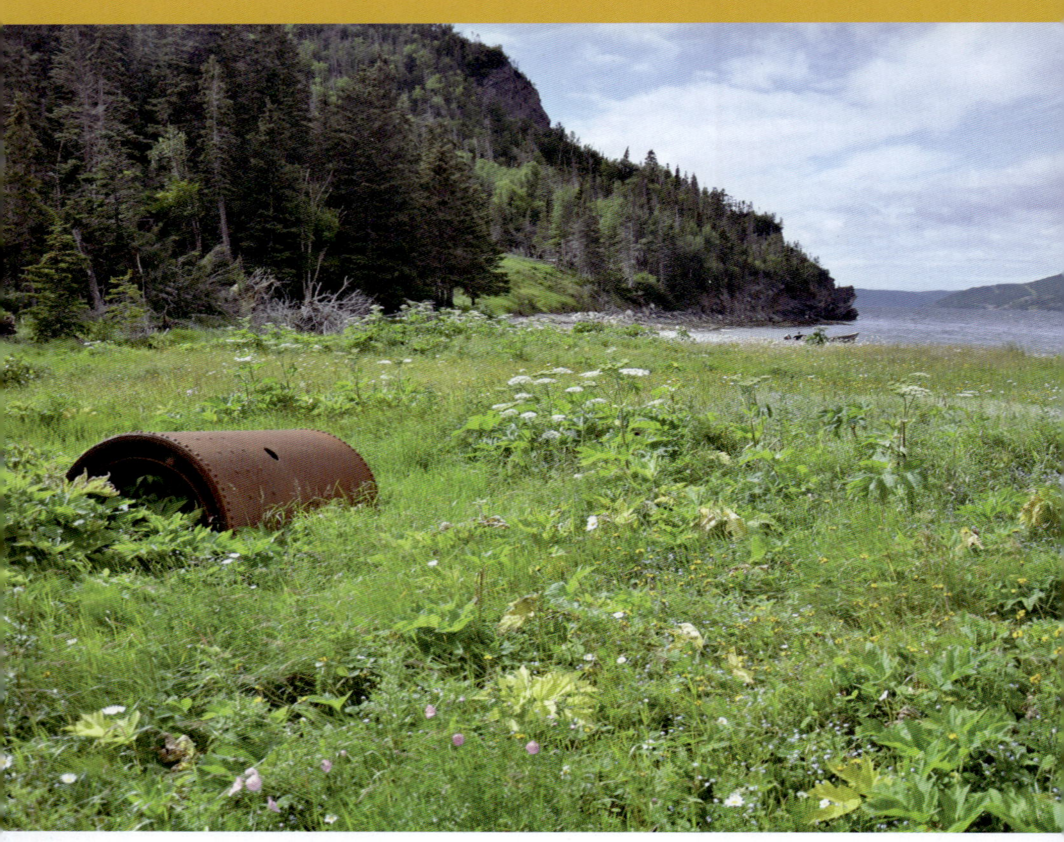

Lomond is located off Route 431 toward Woody Point and Trout River. Approximately 13.5 kilometres from Wiltondale, turn onto a small paved road marked Lomond and Killdevil. Travel along this road for approximately 3.2 kilometres before passing Killdevil Camp and then Lomond. To enter the day park and campground, a park permit is required, which can be purchased at the front gate.

STANLEYVILLE: N 49.466872, W 57.776223

Once in the day park, a trailhead (N 49.460627, W 57.761232) on the far side of the park begins the 2-kilometre trail to Stanleyville. The trail is well maintained but it is a challenging walk.

3. Pissing Mare Falls

Western Brook Pond

Western Brook Pond is one of Newfoundland's best-known tourism destinations. Hidden in the fjord is Pissing Mare Falls, the largest continuous-drop waterfall in Newfoundland and one of the highest continuous-drop waterfalls in Canada.

The waterfall is formed from the runoff of the bogs and ponds that lie on Newfoundland's fourth-highest mountain, known as the Big Level. The water cascades over the cliffside into Western Brook Pond. The waterfall's highest continuous drop is almost 250 metres, with the total height of the waterfall being 343 metres. Unless you tackle the three-day hike along the North Rim Traverse, the only way to see the falls is via the Western Brook Pond boat tour, which operates tours through the gorge during the summer.

PISSING MARE FALLS: N 49.709230, W 57.670154

The falls are located within Western Brook Pond and can only be viewed from the boat tour. Drive 27 kilometres north of Rocky Harbour and park in the lot at the trailhead (N 49.787408, W 57.874607). An easy 3-kilometre walk is required to arrive at the boat tour.

4. Middle Brook Falls & Swimming Hole

Glenburnie, Bonne Bay

Middle Brook Falls is actually three separate falls, each with a swimming hole at its base. The river originates high in the mountains, and the water does not have time to warm up by the time it reaches the falls and swimming hole—but this does not stop the dozens of locals who visit the site each summer from swimming in the frigid waters. The waterfall is set among steep, forested cliffs surrounding the river, and the dark textured rocks over which the falls cascade make for incredible pictures.

The three waterfalls are aptly named First, Second, and Third Falls. The first, the smallest, can hardly be considered anything more than rapids but is a great place for younger children and those who do not consider themselves strong swimmers. Second Falls contains a much larger and deeper pool and a medium waterfall that you can swim up to. The last waterfall, made up of two separate falls, is the biggest of the three. Beneath Third Falls are two deep pools.

⊕ **MIDDLE BROOK FALLS:** N 49.430863, W 57.893481

Access the falls by travelling toward the towns of Woody Point and Trout River on Route 431. Park at Middle Brook Cottages or on the opposite side of Middle Brook Bridge. Walk past the cottages to a small trail that leads down to the river. A short trek along the riverbank will bring you to First Falls. The next two are just around the river bend.

5.   The Old Man

Trout River, Gros Morne National Park

Sitting in the hills behind the picture-perfect town of Trout River is a rock formation known as the Old Man. The rock pillar, located almost 400 metres from the ocean and approximately 20 metres above sea level, is a sea stack formed from coastal erosion 10,000 to 13,000 years ago. Sea levels in the Trout River area are believed to have once been approximately 27 metres higher than they are today. Over thousands of years, the ocean eroded the ancient coastline, creating the sea stack.

The formation resembles a man watching over the community. A short hiking trail takes you close to the Old Man and provides a wonderful view of the community and the ancient sea terrace on which the town was built.

THE OLD MAN: N 49.477753, W 58.133748

The trailhead (N 49.478103, W 58.131351) is on the south side of Trout River on Riverside Drive. From there, a 250-metre maintained trail brings you to the rock formation.

Lighthou
1909

6. Cow Head Lighthouse
Cow Head

This circular 5.5-metre-tall steel lighthouse is perched high on the cliff at the western extremity of the Cow Head Peninsula. It was built in 1909 to aid ships entering Cow Head harbour and those navigating around the rocky peninsula. A lighthouse keeper was stationed at the lighthouse until it was automated in 1960. The light was upgraded several times through its history, and in 1978 became battery operated. In 1988, Transport Canada decommissioned the light, deeming it redundant.

After years of being exposed to the elements, the lighthouse was restored in 2002, and in 2003 was declared a Municipal Heritage Building. It is now maintained regularly and has become a popular hiking destination. The lighthouse offers fantastic views of the coast of Cow Head and Gros Morne.

While hiking to the peninsula, visitors will pass 500-million-year-old rocks that have become the distinctive designation between the Cambrian and Ordovician Periods, as well as several archaeological sites where artifacts have been excavated that once belonged to the Maritime Archaic Indians and Groswater and Dorset Paleo-Eskimos.

◎ **COW HEAD LIGHTHOUSE: N 49.921353, W 57.822740**
Depart from the Cow Head Lighthouse Trail Amphitheatre (N 49.919881, W 57.813581). A 1.5-kilometre hike along a well-maintained trail will bring you to the lighthouse.

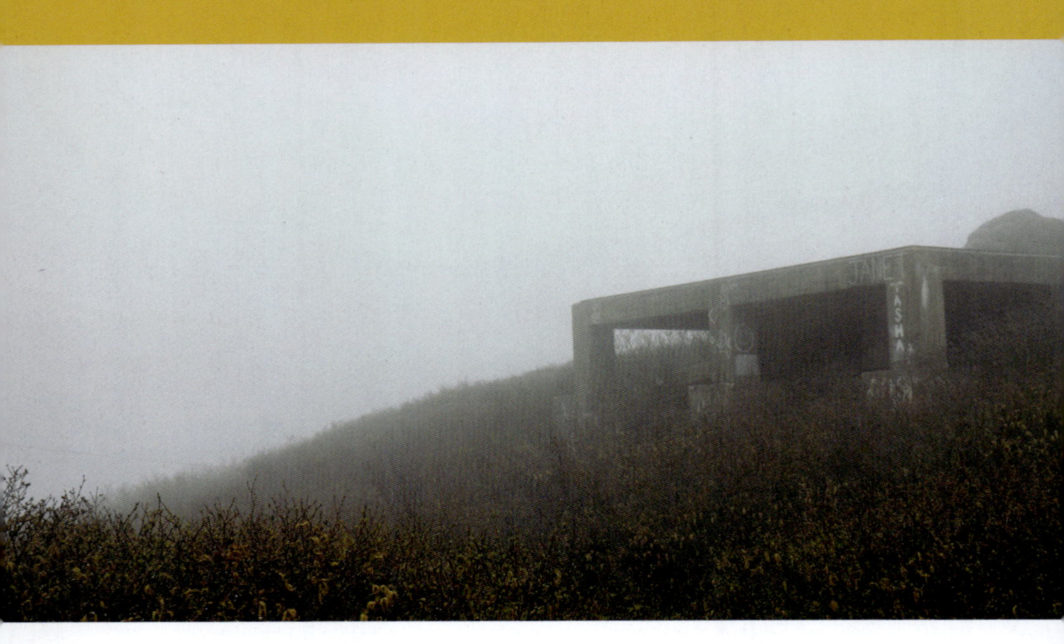

7. St. Anthony Radar Station

St. Anthony

With the radar sites in Logy Bay and Kippens, the St. Anthony Air Station is the third major general surveillance radar station of the Pinetree Line (see pages 156 and 442). Established in November 1953 by the United States Air Force, the site is located on a hill above the town of St. Anthony.

The radar station was placed under the control of the 921st Aircraft Control and Warning Squadron, part of the Northeast Air Command. Its role, as for the other Pinetree Line stations, was to identify enemy aircraft speed, height, and direction, which it would then relay to the Goose Bay Air Force Base. Although no real threat was ever identified, the site was commonly used as a navigational aid for friendly aircraft in the area and answered many search and rescue calls.

Like its counterparts, the site was self-sufficient: it supplied

its own power, water, and living quarters, subsequently turning the hill into a small town. The Aerospace Defense Command took control of the radar station in 1957 and, in the same year, a small gap filler station was constructed near the community of La Scie to extend the coverage of the St. Anthony station. Rapidly changing technology quickly made the La Scie station obsolete; it was decommissioned in 1961. The St. Anthony station operated for another seven years but was decommissioned in 1968 because of the same advancing technology.

While most of the equipment and buildings were removed from the site after it was decommissioned, the concrete foundations for the operations and living quarters, as well as the circular foundation which supported the main radar dome, remain on the hill.

ST. ANTHONY RADAR STATION: N 51.349453, W 55.609680

Drive toward Fishing Point in St. Anthony and turn onto American Drive (located next to Memorial Park, easily identified because of the large Canso water bomber aircraft located in the park). The road is paved for a short distance before turning into gravel. Follow the road for approximately 3.1 kilometres before arriving at the site, on your left.

8. SS *Empire Energy*
Big Brook

Beached on the rocks near the abandoned community of Big Brook on the Northern Peninsula, the wreck of the SS *Empire Energy* is a rusted monument to the risk seafarers took on Newfoundland and Labrador's shores during World War II. Only two sections of hull remain, beached on the rocky shore, but while walking the beach you'll discover a debris field of twisted fragments of this once-great ship.

The wreck is accessible only by travelling some distance on an unmaintained dirt road. For those who trek to it, the wreck is an incredible sight that contrasts with the spectacular scenery found in the Strait of Belle Isle.

HISTORY

The ship was built by Neptun AG in Rostock, Germany, in 1923 and christened *Grete*. The steel-hulled supply ship was 134 metres long and 17 metres wide and had a depth of 9 metres and a draft of 7.8 metres. The 6,570 gross tonnage ship was propelled by a 720-horsepower steam engine, which could propel it up to 20 kilometres per hour.

In 1932, the ship was sold to the Italian firm Achille Lauro & Co. of Naples, Italy, and renamed *Gabbiano*. It was docked in Liverpool, England, until June 10, 1940, when Italy declared war on the UK. Immediately following, the crew members of the Royal Navy ship HMS *Glasgow* stormed aboard the *Gabbiano*, seizing the ship and its civilian crew as prisoners of war.

The ship was then taken over by the Ministry of War Transport,

where it joined a group of merchant supply ships that made up the Merchant Navy. All ships in the group were named *Empire* followed by a word beginning with E. The renamed *Empire Energy* began delivering supplies to England from the coast of Africa, Iceland, the US, and Canada.

The ship's final chapter began when it docked in Sydney, Nova Scotia, to await the departure of a protective military convoy. On October 29, 1941, the *Empire Energy* joined Convoy SC.52 and embarked east on a voyage around the northeast coast of Newfoundland. As the convoy reached the north coast of Newfoundland, the risk of U-boat attack forced the US Navy Department to order the convoy back to Sydney via the quickest route, through the Strait of Belle Isle.

On November 3, as the convoy headed for the Strait, U-boat U-123 spotted the convoy and relayed its position to four U-boats nearby. As the convoy neared Notre Dame Bay, it was attacked, resulting in the sinking of the steamers *Flynderborg* and *Gretavale*. As the convoy approached Cape Charles, the *Empire Gemsbuck* was also sunk.

The escort commander aboard the HMS *Broadway* was not able to defend all the ships in the convoy against the U-boats and ordered the ships to disperse and make their own way through the Strait. In the early morning of November 4, the *Empire Energy* ran aground. Deteriorating weather and sea conditions forced the ship onto the rocks near Big Brook, Newfoundland. In his book *The History of Canada Series: War in the St. Lawrence*, Roger Sarty states that the *Empire Energy* was never categorized as a German victory by western sources; however, there is little doubt that the direct actions and threat of German U-boats caused the sinking of this supply ship. As such, the *Empire Energy* is considered by some to be the first German victory in the Gulf of St. Lawrence.

The ship's damage was irreparable and it was quickly declared a total loss. Its cargo, a large shipment of food consisting primarily of corn, was deemed not worth saving. But while the ship and cargo were not saved, everyone on board survived, thanks to the quick rescue efforts of locals and other ships in the area.

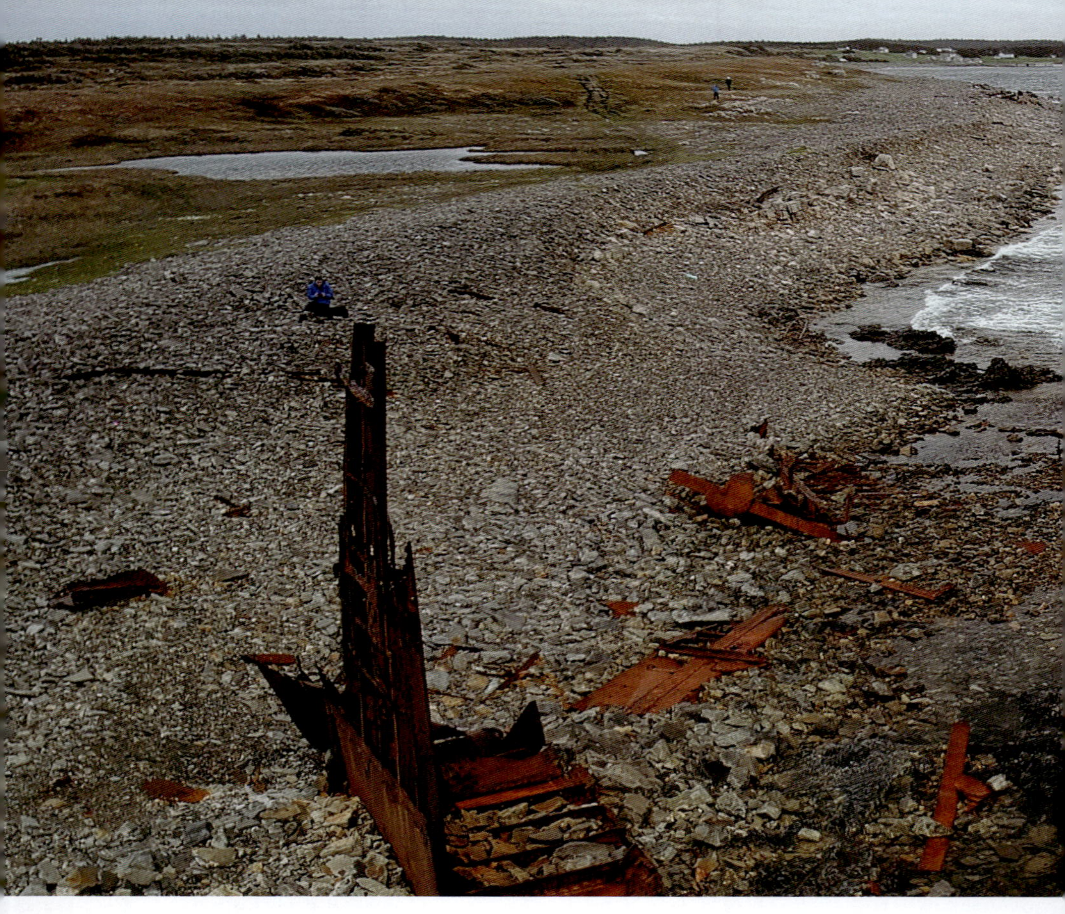

Today the rusted hull of the ship rests on the shallow rocky shores of the Strait of Belle Isle. The ship is a spectacle and one of the larger shipwrecks visible in the province today. Its hull has deteriorated greatly over the past decades, likely due to seasonal ice floes. The main hull stands tall out of the water, while, to the north, a debris field of rusting metal components litters the coast. The ship is backdropped by the barren coastline of the Northern Peninsula. Just south of the wreck is the abandoned community of Big Brook.

 **SS EMPIRE ENERGY:** N 51.528546, W 56.134896

Access to the wreck site is located off Route 435 approximately 9.4 kilometres south of the community of Cook's Harbour (N 51.536706, W 55.939642). Travelling about 15 kilometres on an unmaintained dirt road will bring you near the abandoned community of Big Brook. A 250-metre walk to the coast will bring you to the wreck site. The route can be easily travelled by ATV or off-road vehicles.

9. Big Brook

Northern Peninsula

Big Brook is a small, abandoned fishing community on the northeast shore of the Northern Peninsula. Big Brook is nestled in a small, forested cove at the mouth of a brook by the same name. The town first appeared on a census in 1874 when a reported nine people between two families were living there. While the area provided close access to fishing grounds in Labrador and the Strait of Belle Isle, the community remained small because of its remoteness and harsh weather conditions.

By 1970, the community was connected by a highway constructed to join the town of St. Anthony with the rest of the province. This did little to change the population of the town and, as it dwindled, the Government of Newfoundland and Labrador decided to resettle the 10 permanent residents in 2004.

After this, the road leading to the community was no longer maintained. While it is in relatively good shape as of 2021, the bridge crossing Big Brook has been removed. The only way into the community by vehicle is now from Cook's Harbour to the north.

BIG BROOK: N 51.520133, W 56.150061

The community is located on the old, unpaved Northern Peninsula highway. There are two points of access: in the south (N 51.412913, W 56.448707) and the north (N 51.536740, W 55.939763). The southern access point is in the town of Eddies Cove; the northern access through Cook's Harbour (Route 435). A travel distance of 24 kilometres or 16 kilometres is required, respectively.

10. Hand-Built Ships of Bide Arm

Roddickton-Bide Arm

Boatbuilding has always been part of Newfoundland tradition, dating to before Europeans settled the land. Sadly, this tradition is slowly fading away. Nowhere demonstrates this better than in Bide Arm, where the incredible works of art that are Lod Rowsell's hand-built boats reside.

Pushed ashore and in disrepair, the collection includes a 9-metre-long fishing sloop (a single mast boat), a small punt, and a 12-metre-long replica of *The Matthew*. Although each year they deteriorate a little more, they continue to serve as a reminder and memorial to the magnificent hand-built boats that once sailed along our coasts.

BIDE ARM: N 50.806986, W 56.102752

From Route 433, turn onto Main Street toward the small town of Bide Arm. Drive to the end of this road for the best viewing of the incredible hand-built ships.

11. The Underground Salmon River
Roddickton, Northern Peninsula

Three main sections of Beaver Brook on the Northern Peninsula are a must-see. The first is where water from the main brook is diverted into a narrow gorge. Here, large logs and debris from the river swirl around continuously as the river plunges underground. Seventy-five metres away, the river is forced upward into a small pond that is most likely a collapsed section of the cave system through which the river flows. From there, the water makes its way underground one more time for approximately 185 metres before exiting and rejoining the main channel. The unique underground river system was formed from the slow erosion of the limestone bedrock.

The river is one of the only known places in the world where salmon travel underground to get to their spawning grounds. This provides the section of the river with its more common name, the underground salmon river. Each year during the summer months, hundreds of salmon swim up the river and through the cave system before continuing their journey farther upstream.

A beautiful trail system weaves through the forested area and brings visitors to each section of the underground river. Although the park is advertised and maintained, this geologic and ecologic wonder is far too often forgotten or neglected.

The underground salmon river is one of Newfoundland's most awe-inspiring places. Be sure to include it in your travels to the Great Northern Peninsula.

The turnoff to the underground salmon river is approximately 9 kilometres north of Roddickton off Route 433. From there, a 2.5-kilometre dirt road will bring you to the trailhead. A well-maintained, 1.0-kilometre walking trail brings you through the area.

12. Conche Harbour Lighthouse
Conche

The quaint lighthouse in beautiful Conche was built in 1914. The pyramidal wood tower sits 4 metres high at the entrance of Conche harbour. It was used until 1992, when the light was transferred to a new tower built a little farther offshore. At the time, the small wooden structure was in disrepair, but it was rebuilt and restored by volunteers in the community.

In 2021, the lighthouse stands at the base of the fjord on which the town of Conche sits. Even though the lighthouse may

not be enough of a reason to drive over the gravel highway, the town is. It is easily one of the most picturesque and overlooked communities in Newfoundland and Labrador.

 **CONCHE HARBOUR LIGHTHOUSE:** N 50.885843, W 55.897211

From the town of Roddickton, travel about 26 kilometres on Route 434 to Conche. The lighthouse is in the centre of the community near the local marina and fish plant.

13. Conche Plane Crash

Conche

Lying in the grassy fields behind the small town of Conche is the wreckage of a Douglas DB-7 plane. The unusual site does not appear to match the quiet, picturesque landscape, but in 1942 the ill-fated aircraft brought the ongoing war to the shores of the town.

The story of the wreck begins in Gander on November 30, 1942. The Royal Canadian Air Force plane, code-named BZ-277, was being piloted by Squadron Leader Robert Morrow, accompanied by radio operator Flight Sergeant McLaughlin, and navigator Pilot Officer Tamhlym when it took off just after 8 a.m. It was a regular flight across the Atlantic to deliver the plane and pilot to England. Because of the plane's small fuel capacity, the crew planned to land in Greenland for refuelling before continuing to the UK. As the plane flew over the Northern Peninsula, it was forced to make a crash landing, likely due to either a fuel shortage or ice buildup. The pilot put the plane down in the relatively flat fields in Conche,

crashing through several fences before coming to a stop near the place where it sits today.

Luckily, the crew survived, with only minor injuries, including the navigator, who bailed out of the plane early due to his seat in the nose of the plane. The people of Conche heard the crash and quickly arrived to aid the three men. The coastal ship *L.K. Sweeney* was sent to begin salvaging the wreckage. The plane's sensitive equipment and gear were dismantled and loaded on board, while the fuselage, wings, and outer shell were left in the grassy field.

The crash site is fenced off, with interpretive signs erected to share the story of that unfortunate day. It is a National Historic Site.

⊕ **CONCHE PLANE CRASH:** N 50.882714, W 55.893140

This is one of the most accessible plane crash sites on the island. The trailhead (N 50.883571, W 55.892380) is located off Martinique Drive in Conche; the wreckage is at the end of a short well-maintained trail.

14. Glass Hole

Conche

Hidden along the cliffs near the picturesque town of Conche is the Glass Hole. Piercing through the southern ridge of the Conche Peninsula, Glass Hole is a naturally formed arch approximately 79 metres tall and 10 metres wide, and, at its most extreme, produces a hole approximately 30 metres in height.

The geomorphic feature was carved over tens of thousands of years by erosion of the cliff face. It is made of fine-grained sandstone, siltstone, and shale and is part of the Cape Rouge Formation. These weak rocks were formed 359 to 347 million years ago and twisted and folded into the ridge visible today. Each year, storms and strong waves eroded the ridge, which initially would have formed a cave before collapsing, opening up this hole in the mountain. This formation story makes it difficult to classify the Glass Hole as either a cave or an arch; either way, it earns a position on the list of the province's unique geologic wonders.

Glass Hole has another hidden feature: fossils. Exploring the rock face and surrounding rock outcrops reveals fossils of plants and organisms that existed at the time the rocks were formed. Ridges, bumps, and indentations are the remains of an environment from 350 million years ago.

The small town of Conche has developed a series of trails and pathways that allow visitors to easily access the arch and also enjoy the beauty of the Conche Peninsula. While visiting, be sure to watch for whales, birds, and icebergs. The area holds some of the best accessible views of the eastern Northern Peninsula.

GLASS HOLE: N 50.864447, W 55.889151

The trail to Glass Hole begins in Conche near the location of the 1942 plane crash (N 50.883571, W 55.892380). From there, a moderately difficult, 6.8-kilometre loop trail follows the east side of the Conche Peninsula to the arch.

15. Lost Airstrips of the Northern Peninsula

Portland Creek, Main Brook, & Cook's Harbour

Although boat travel has always been the primary mode of transporting people and goods to the nooks and crannies of Newfoundland, it had its limitations. Throughout the 1960s, 1970s, and 1980s, the provincial government invested in the construction

of airstrips to allow for better accessibility to Newfoundland's isolated communities. As highways and roads were constructed, however, the need for an airstrip in every community diminished. As time went on, many of these airstrips were left to deteriorate.

As you travel through the northern reaches of the province, the remains of these runways can still be found. In Portland Creek, the Sperry Gyroscope Company from Great Neck, New York, constructed an 850-metre airstrip to exploit the fishing and hunting potential in the interior of the peninsula. The airstrip proved successful in driving the province's hunting and fishing tourism with American and Canadian sportsmen, an industry that continues today. The airstrip's use dwindled over time and, by the late 1980s, was only used for an occasional emergency flight or landing. The airstrip, eventually allowed to grow over, was later purchased for the establishment of a campground and day park, which remains there in 2021.

Similar to the runways at Portland Creek are the abandoned runways located near the communities of Cook's Harbour and Main Brook. While they no longer possess the importance they once did, these runways remain an important reminder of attempts to connect the people and families of Newfoundland's remote communities.

PORTLAND CREEK: N 50.194356, W 57.589508

MAIN BROOK: N 51.129579, W 55.988272

COOK'S HARBOUR: N 51.494424, W 55.819662

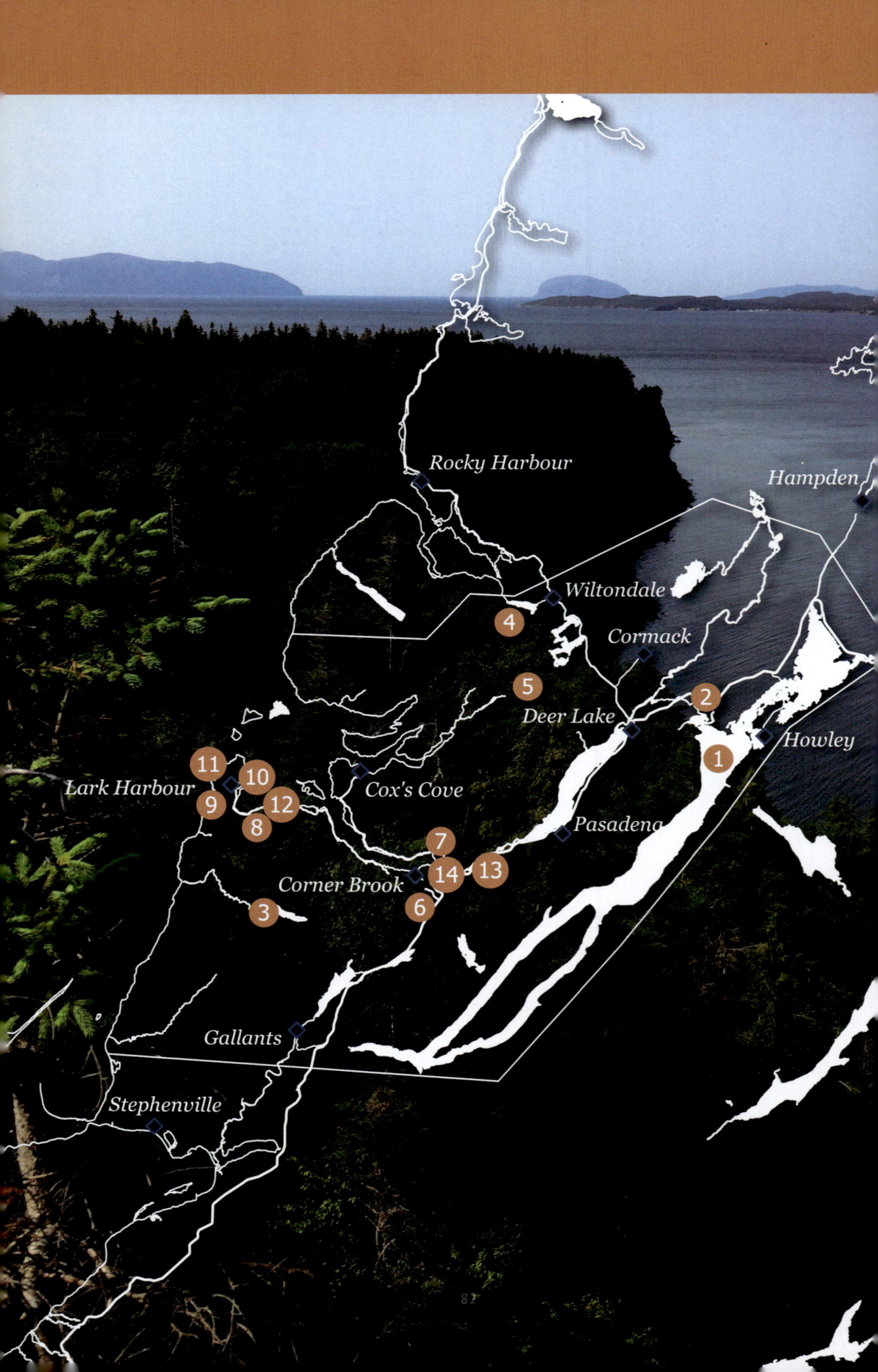

Rocky Harbour
Hampden
Wiltondale
Cormack
4
5
2
Deer Lake
Howley
1
11
10
Lark Harbour
Cox's Cove
9
12
8
7
Pasadena
14
13
Corner Brook
6
3
Gallants
Stephenville

West Coast

Serpentine Valley, Bay of Islands, & Deer Lake

The west coast is nestled among the Long Range Mountains and backdropped by the ophiolite complexes that are the towering Northern Arm Hills, Blow Me Down Mountains, and Newfoundland's highest mountain, the Cabox in the Lewis Hills. Separating the peaks are the glacier-carved valleys and rolling, forested hills that make up the dramatic topography surrounding Corner Brook. The communities in this region are new relative to the rest of the island and today rely on forestry and tourism to keep them going.

While some west coast settlements were established throughout the 19th century, it was not until the Newfoundland Railway was built at the end of that century that the region began expanding. The onshore and Labrador fisheries were crucial to the first communities. Several mining operations were established but did not have the impact of the forestry and logging industries.

In 1925, the opening of the Corner Brook Pulp and Paper Mill and its hydroelectric facility in Deer Lake provided an economic boom. A vast network of logging roads was created, used now by ATV enthusiasts, hunters, and hikers. These roads make the region one of the top snowmobile destinations in the world. Fishing,

forestry, and government services are the main employers in the region in 2021; the towns of Corner Brook and Deer Lake act as service hubs for the many communities on the island's west coast and throughout the Northern Peninsula.

The largely uninhabited west coast is best explored by hiking, snowmobile, or ATV. But those travelling by road-going vehicles need not miss out. The Trans-Canada Highway traverses the centre of the region, winding through Corner Brook and

the scenic Humber Valley as it moves through the Long Range Mountains. From Corner Brook, Routes 450 and 440 travel along the north and south sides of Humber Arm respectively, providing an expansive view of both Humber Arm and the Blow Me Down Mountains. Farther north, Deer Lake is considered the gateway to the north, and travelling farther east along the Trans-Canada Highway, Route 420 connects the communities of Howley and Grand Lake to the rest of the island.

1. Grand Lake

Western Newfoundland

Grand Lake is Newfoundland's largest and deepest lake. A stretch of fresh water nearly 100 kilometres long and likely over 300 metres deep. The lake meets sandy beaches, hummocky terrain, and low, rolling hills at its north end. Farther south, these hills turn into mountains and the lake is split by an enormous island bordered by pine-forested cliffs and plunging waterfalls. At each side of the island are deep fjords rivalling those in Western Brook Pond (page 51).

Grand Lake was created by tectonic forces, inland glaciers, and the pulp and paper industry that funneled wealth and brought permanent settlements to the west coast. Above and below Grand Lake are wonders, many yet undiscovered, including waterfalls, fjords, shipwrecks, submerged towns, and possibly a lost culture.

GEOLOGIC HISTORY

Most of the rocks that make up the region are between 350 and 550 million years old, some even older. Grand Lake is situated along the Cabot fault line, which loosely separates the west coast, a geologic region called the Humber Zone, from the Dunnage Zone to the east. Over millions of years, these two regions collided, creating the complex geology present today.

During the ice age, several large glaciers covered what is now Newfoundland's west coast. Ice gouged the fjords and hilltops, creating roughly the current topography. As the glaciers receded 10,000 to 12,000 years ago, a large lake was formed that makes up most of today's Grand Lake, Sandy Lake, and Birchy Lake. That

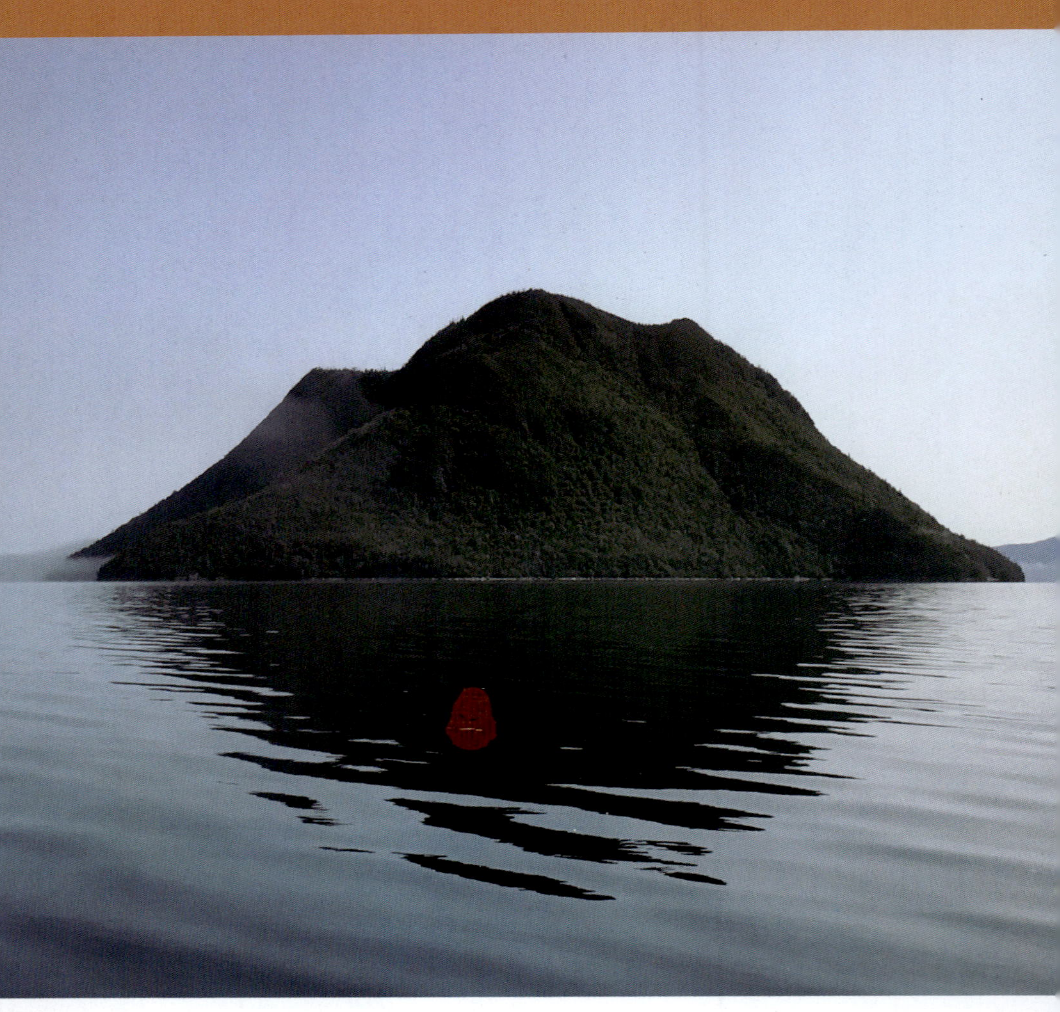

lake drained through Harry's River in the south.

Over time, elevation changes in the land from melting glaciers produced new routes for water to flow. Eventually, water found its way out through Junction Brook, where it flowed until 1925. This new spillway lowered the lake level dramatically, and during initial release the flow rate is believed to have been almost five times greater than that of Niagara Falls.

As these dramatic changes slowed, new vegetation flourished and the landscape soon stabilized.

HUMAN INFLUENCE

The first humans to live near Grand Lake were the Beothuk and Mi'kmaq. After European colonization of the island, the population of Indigenous peoples decreased as white settlers pushed farther west. The construction of the Newfoundland Railway and transportation routes in the late 19th century and early 20th century led to new industries on the west coast. Construction of the Corner Brook Pulp and Paper mill began in 1923. It would become the largest in the world and to power it water from Newfoundland's largest lake was essential.

Grand Lake had just one outlet through a narrow river valley containing Junction Brook. To harness the hydro power, a large diversion dam, known as Main Dam (page 94), was constructed between 1922 and 1925. Once complete, the 225-metre-long, 23-metre-high structure raised the lake depth.

Raising the water level brought the level of Grand Lake to that of nearby Sandy Lake and Birchy Lake, creating essentially one connected lake and submerging the rivers that flowed between them. Small islands throughout the lakes, parts of the community of Howley, the existing railway line, and the dam's construction site all flooded. The shores of the lake where the Beothuk were known to live and fish were also flooded, possibly erasing useful archeological evidence of their culture and way of life.

ABOUT THE AREA

Grand Lake is a vast inland body of water found on the eastern edge of Newfoundland's west coast. If you include the connected water bodies of Sandy Lake and Birchy Lake (which have the same water elevation), you can travel nearly 140 kilometres without

going through any rivers or rapids. On each end, it offers very different landscapes. To the south, the lake narrows due to the presence of Glover Island, a 38-kilometre-long, 5.5-kilometre-wide island whose steep cliffs produce spectacular fjords on either side, but most notably the northwestern side. The lake and its surrounding hills mark the transition between Central Newfoundland and the Long Range Mountains.

THE ODDITIES CREATED FROM FLOODING

The construction of Main Dam and the flooding of Grand Lake gave the lake unusual qualities. Within the fjord created by Grand Lake and Glover Island are dozens of large waterfalls that spill over the steep edges and cliffs. In countless places, smaller brooks wind through narrow gullies and crevasses cut into the cliffs before falling into the lake. Typically, when waterfalls and rivers enter lakes, suspended sediment and rocks and gravel moved by the water create deltas and beaches, which over time build up to slow the water as it enters the larger water body. When Grand Lake was flooded, however, these deltas and beaches were submerged, that is, many of the waterfalls along Grand Lake's shores fall directly into the lake. Only those in canoes, kayaks, and other boats can get extremely close to these waterfalls.

This feature, combined with the high number of waterfalls found along this stretch, creates one of the most abundant areas for waterfalls on the island.

The flooding of Grand Lake also resulted in remarkable losses: islands, shoreline, infrastructure, buildings, roads, and railways. Best seen at the southern end of the lake, a submerged 100-year-old forest makes the area extremely dangerous to boats and recreational users. Large pine and spruce trees are still visible, planted into the lake bed and rising to the surface. Each year some of these large trees break free from their underwater routes and float throughout the lake before washing ashore.

Near Main Dam, the piers of the original Junction Brook railway bridge, the large wooden cofferdam used in the construction of the dam and other structures, is visible just several metres below the surface of the water.

Several sunken and run-aground barges are found around the lake. These relics are left over from when the lake was used as a transportation network for logging. Logs were cut, placed on the lake, and towed to canals, where they flowed to the hydroelectric facility in Deer Lake before continuing to the mill in Corner Brook.

The easiest access to Grand Lake is in the town of Howley, at its northern end, which offers beautiful views and beaches. Use the region's logging roads to access the lake's southern end and western side.

HOWLEY:

Approximately 30 kilometres east of Deer Lake on the Trans-Canada Highway, turn onto Route 401 and drive 14 kilometres to Howley. The Grand Lake Tourist Park (N 49.159712, W 57.119522) and the old railway trestle bridge (N 49.164824, W 57.131403) are the best spots to launch a boat or view the lake.

SOUTH END OF LAKE:

Approximately 37 kilometres south of Corner Brook on the Trans-Canada Highway, turn onto a gravel road across the highway from Route 402 to Gallants. Drive approximately 4.8 kilometres to the south end of the lake and local cabin community.

NORTH HARBOUR:

On the west side of the town of Pasadena, turn onto Adams Crescent and continue for 300 metres. The road turns to gravel and becomes North Harbour Road. Continue along the deteriorated road for about 14 kilometres before arriving at the charming little harbour on the lake.

While numerous gravel roads provide vantage points of the lake, the best way to experience the lake is by boat. But the lake's isolation and unpredictable weather create dangerous conditions for those unfamiliar with the area.

2. Main Dam

Junction Brook, Grand Lake

Holding back the weight of Grand Lake is Main Dam. Rising above Junction Brook, west of Deer Lake, the 23.3-metre-tall structure was an outstanding engineering achievement and continues to be an impressive symbol of Newfoundland and Labrador's pulp and paper industry.

HISTORY

In the early 1920s, the west coast's power infrastructure was severely lacking. To power the newly built Corner Brook Pulp and Paper mill,

Newfoundland Power and Paper built a massive concrete dam on Junction River to divert water through a newly excavated 11-kilometre-long canal to a powerhouse near Deer Lake.

The dam was constructed by the firm W.I. Bishop and completed in 1925. An Ambursen style dam, it has a large sloped concrete slab on the upstream side supported by vertical walls, or buttresses. This design uses minimal concrete and resources but provides the strength required to hold back 8 million cubic metres of water in Grand Lake.

The structure is 225.6 metres wide and 23.3 metres tall. Eighteen 4.7-metre-wide steel gates span the length of the dam and are opened by one of the two gantry cranes located atop the dam. When the gates are open, the dam can discharge approximately 1,840 cubic metres of water per second into the Junction Brook Spillway. This water flows through the gates and over the front of the dam before being redirected into the air by "flip-bucket" deflectors at the bottom of the dam, preventing excessive erosion at the dam's base.

The dam is still being used to supply power in 2021 by the Corner Brook Pulp and Paper Mill. The best time to visit is during high-water levels, when the dam's gates are opened to discharge excess water.

 **MAIN DAM:** N 49.198247, W 57.256695

Main Dam is not difficult to access via snowmobile, ATV, bicycle, or snowshoes. The old Newfoundland Railway line (now the Newfoundland T'Railway) crosses over the top of the dam and is the easiest and most common route to it by snowmobile, bicycle, or ATV.

Off-road Vehicle/ATV/Bicycle:

Access the Newfoundland T'Railway near Deer Lake (N 49.174432, W 57.416462) and travel east approximately 13 kilometres to the dam, or depart from Howley (N 49.166077, W 57.121450) and travel westward along the T'Railway for approximately 11.5 kilometres.

Hike/Snowshoe:

Depart from the Crooked Feeder Bridge located on the Trans-Canada Highway east of Deer Lake and trek 2.3 kilometres over Mary Ann's Bog to the Newfoundland T'Railway. Travel a further 1.5 kilometres west to the dam.

Even though hiking is the shortest route to the dam, crossing the bog in the summer can be wet and strenuous. During the winter, the bog freezes, offering snowshoeing or cross-country skiing and backcountry access to beautiful scenery and caribou herds that call the bog home in the winter.

3. Serpentine Valley
South of Bay of Islands

Located south of the Bay of Islands is the picturesque Serpentine Valley. This valley lies between the Blow Me Down Mountains and the island's largest mountains, Lewis Hills. In the valley is the 10-kilometre-long Serpentine Lake. Many small rivers flow through the dramatic valleys and fjords of both mountains.

The area is a popular destination for hikers and snowmobilers and is easiest to access in the winter via snowmobile. For years, logging in this area has resulted in many dirt roads; these are maintained by local cabin owners.

A PEOPLE'S HISTORY

Although Serpentine Valley is believed to have originally been inhabited by the Mi'kmaq, the first record of people settling there dates to 1884. These people occupied the mouth of the Serpentine River and made a living fishing salmon and cod. Interest in the area grew in 1898 when the Newfoundland Railway was constructed several kilometres to the west.

This area gained popularity not only for its abundant fish stocks but also when the Corner Brook mill was constructed and logging increased. It soon became a well-known fishing and hunting location for loggers and, eventually, for American servicepeople stationed at the nearby air force base in Stephenville.

In 1934, the Serpentine Valley became one of the first areas of Newfoundland considered for a national park. Although this idea was eventually abandoned, interest in developing the area for tourism has remained.

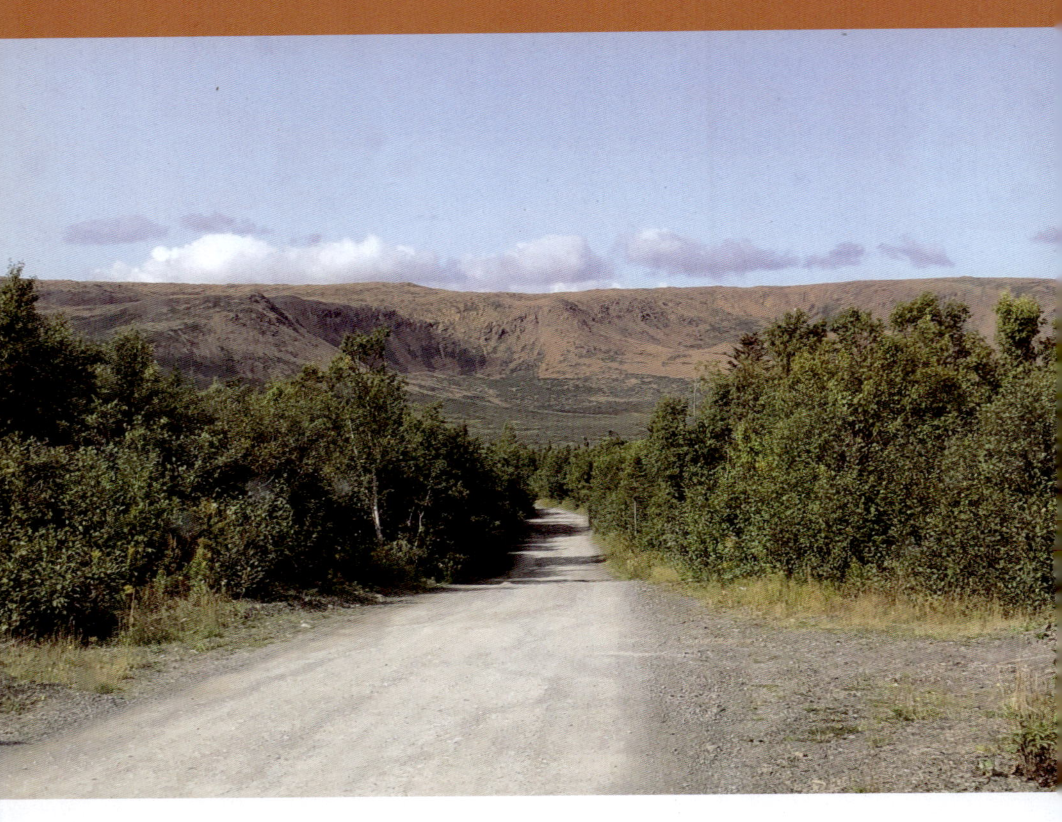

HISTORY OF THE LANDSCAPE

The Serpentine Valley, carved by glaciers, rests between the two ophiolite massifs of Lewis Hills and Blow Me Down Mountains. For those who do not speak rocks, ophiolite means a section of oceanic crust and upper mantle that was uplifted and left exposed as a whole or "massif" structure on the present-day earth's surface.

The Lewis Hills—specifically the peak known as The Cabox, elevation of 814 metres—are the highest mountains on the island of Newfoundland. The flat-topped mountains are comprised of mainly mafic and ultramafic rocks. Similar to rocks found in the Tablelands of Gros Morne, the ultramafic rock that makes up the area of the mountain closest to the valley is known as peridotite.

Peridotite gives the mountains a distinct rust colour; this is one of the few places in the world where this mantle-derived rock is found. These mountains formed in two different periods between 541 million and 485 million years ago.

On the northside of the valley are the prominent Blow Me Down Mountains. These 750-metre-tall mountains developed in a way similar to the Lewis Hills. From within the valley the colour of these mountains changes in the east-west direction; the ultramafic peridotite at the eastern section of the mountain quickly changes to mafic oceanic crust, signified by a darker, more vegetated landscape. Similar to the mafic rocks located on the south side of the Lewis Hills, these rocks consist mainly of gabbro and other igneous rocks with high magnesium and iron contents.

Both mountains are scattered with signs of millions of years of erosion. Deep, plunging fjords, sharp pointy peaks, and steep ridges known as aretes are the remnants of the glaciers that eroded and formed the Serpentine Valley. Large waterfalls, meandering rivers, and evidence of large landslides are modern-day reminders that these mountains are still changing.

ABOUT THE AREA

Not only does this area require a significant investment of time to explore, it also requires the ability to do so. The valley is easiest viewed on a snowmobile as numerous snowmobile trails wind through the hills and valleys surrounding Serpentine Lake. In the summer, the region's logging roads provide access for those with ATVs or vehicles capable of travelling long distances on gravel roads. If you are new to the area, consult with local tour guides for the best options.

 ### SERPENTINE LOOKOUT

View the mountains and lake from a little-known lookout atop a hill on the eastern end of the lake (N 48.876919, W 58.169127).

 ### LAKESIDE BEACH

At the western reach of Serpentine Lake and the start of the Serpentine River is a small beach and low-lying area which provides views of the lake and surrounding mountains (N 48.893987, W 58.320527).

Getting to the valley requires an ATV, snowmobile, off-road vehicle, or a multiday hike. If you are unfamiliar with the area, consult with local guides or tour operators who can provide the information required to complete the trip. See Exploring Further (page 473) for resources and area maps.

Hiking

No maintained trails exist through the area, but the Newfoundland and Labrador chapter of the International Appalachian Trail (www.iatnl.com) has produced a hiking route through the valley and over both the Lewis Hills and Blow Me Down Mountains.

Snowmobile

Although no groomed trail network travels through the valley, several side routes regularly used by snowmobilers and cabin owners allow access to the lake and surrounding area. Consult with the Newfoundland and Labrador Snowmobile Federation and the local snowmobile club, the Western Sno-Riders, for more information on trails, maps, and current conditions. If you are travelling on the groomed trail system, you must purchase a trail pass from the local snowmobile club.

ATV/Off-road Vehicle

A huge network of current and past logging roads exists in the area. No one resource identifies the road network or conditions, but resources such as the Provincial Land Use Atlas and Geoatlas can help identify routes and roads.

Contact Rugged Edge in Corner Brook for snowmobile and ATV rentals and tours.

4. Lomond Sinkhole

Lomond

Tucked away in the forested hills behind the camping community of Lomond is an enormous sinkhole, approximately 30 metres deep and 45 metres wide. The magnificence of the sinkhole is lost in pictures. Inside the vertical-sided hole, a waterfall cascades into the centre, disappearing into the rocks below. No one is sure of its outlet, but it is possible that it enters an unexplored cave system that flows out into the Lomond River. Although the Lomond Sinkhole has become a popular destination for snowmobilers and hikers over the last several years, it remains one of the most spectacular places to visit on the island.

GEOLOGIC HISTORY

Sinkholes form when weak carbonate-rich rock (commonly limestone or dolomite) erodes beneath the ground due to water percolation from the surface or groundwater flow. Water dissolves the carbonate in the rocks, producing voids or pockets of air beneath the ground. Once enough rock has eroded, a cave forms, and over time, the roof of the cave might collapse, creating a collapsed sinkhole.

Much of Newfoundland's water is stored in bogs and stagnant ponds, which causes increased acidity. In the case of the Lomond Sinkhole, this acidic water seeped through a vertical fault and eroded a weak layer of limestone located beneath a stronger layer of slate. Over time, this erosion created a cave, until it collapsed, creating the large depression we see today.

As logging in the Lomond area has been ongoing for over 100 years, it is likely that the first people to stumble upon the sinkhole were loggers. One of the earliest people believed to have used the land around the sinkhole was Cyril Goosney, who logged the area in 1957 for Bowater's pulp and paper mill. Logs and rotting timber found at the bottom of the sinkhole are believed to be remnants of this first operation.

The most recent logging in the area was by Corner Brook Pulp and Paper in 2010. The area was clear-cut, producing the current barren landscape. At this time, the company placed an informative sign at the top of the sinkhole and created a 20-metre-wide buffer surrounding the hole for safety.

ABOUT THE AREA

The sinkhole's location in the hilly terrain has prevented it from becoming a major tourist attraction. But those who know where to look are greeted with a view of this wonder.

 **LOMOND SINKHOLE: N 49.364149, W 57.716347**

The sinkhole is relatively easy to access. While the most common way to reach it is by snowmobile in the winter, it is also accessible via hiking or by an off-road vehicle.

Off-road Vehicle/ATV/Snowmobile

Begin on White Wash Road (N 49.365630, W 57.582011), a dirt road located off Route 430 just north of Bonne Bay Pond. Travel on this well-used dirt road for approximately 6 kilometres, then turn right onto a small dirt road (N 49.328013, W 57.630759). Travel another 3.1 kilometres, then turn right onto the next road (N 49.324608, W 57.670312). Continue for approximately 7.5 kilometres to another small road off to the left (N 49.364854, W 57.715759). Park your vehicle and walk the remaining 200 metres to the rim of the sinkhole (N 49.364149, W 57.716347).

Hike/Snowshoe

The trailhead is located immediately off Route 431 (N 49.402834, W 57.730214). Leaving from the trailhead along the highway, walk about 300 metres, then turn left onto a small gravel road named Tower Road. Hike approximately 4.7 kilometres to a clear-cut section of road (N 49.371304, W 57.716815). From here, hike approximately 700 metres south across the clear-cut to the sinkhole (N 49.364149, W 57.716347).

5. Sinkholes & Disappearing Streams

Western Newfoundland

The Lomond Sinkhole is a type of karst topography, which describes features that have been carved and formed by the dissolution or erosion of soluble rocks such as limestone or dolomite. This type of topography is relatively rare in Newfoundland and Labrador and is characterized by sinkholes, caves, and underground water passages.

The landscape enclosed by the Bay of Islands, Gros Morne National Park, and Deer Lake is highly influenced by karst topography, with features formed from the erosion of weak limestone rock that spread across the region. This rock dates to the Cambrian and Ordovician periods (approximately 540 to 470 million years ago) and is the remnant of an ancient ocean known as the Iapetus Ocean. For millions of years, organisms lived and died in the area, accumulating on the shallow ocean floor. Over time, they were buried, and eventually plate tectonics shifted and twisted the rock. Over millions of years, erosion shaped and eroded the rocks. This was especially prevalent in the last several hundred thousand years, where constant glaciation periods moulded the landscape and its features into what we see now.

While the area has been regularly logged over the past 50 years, most of it remains unexposed and thus holds vast exploration potential. An unknown number of underground streams, cave systems, and sinkholes exist, making this a fascinating area to explore. Below are some of the places that can be found alongside the Lomond Sinkhole.

Northwest of the cabin community of Lomond is another sinkhole. This feature is not as large in diameter as the Lomond Sinkhole but is about the same depth. There is no easy way down or out of it due to the steep vertical cliffs. For many years, the people who live in the region believed this to be the only sinkhole; it was not until Bowater began logging the area that the Lomond Sinkhole became known.

As is the case with the other Lomond Sinkhole, the outlet of this hole is unknown; however, many believe that it discharges into the Lomond River located approximately 2 kilometres away. This sinkhole's relatively small diameter helps hide it from even those who travel alongside it on snowmobile or ATV. Nonetheless, this 4.5-kilometre hike (one-way) is improved by the beauty of the thick old-growth forest in which it is hidden.

 **LOMOND SINKHOLE #2:** N 49.390725, W 57.766707
The trailhead is located off Route 431 on a small dirt road (N 49.402750, W 57.730279). Travel along the dirt road for approximately 4.5 kilometres to the sinkhole. Attention is required to navigate through the area's many trails; however, the small dirt road is relatively easy to traverse.

UNDERGROUND BROOK

Bonne Bay Pond

Located on the side of Route 430 in a small cove on Bonne Bay Pond, water rises to the surface into a small, sectioned-off part of the lake. What you see is the outflow of a large river that flows underground for approximately 900 metres. At the entrance, the water quickly drops over a small waterfall into a steep, rock-lined channel. At the bottom of this gorge is a small bottomless lake where the river enters its underground pathway. The unusual and dramatic gorge may also be a form of sinkhole—but what can be said for certain is that the gorge is worth the 20-minute walk for anyone interested in the world beneath their feet. The entrance of the river is spectacular, but so is the exit, located along Route 430 and best seen during high runoff, where water bubbles to the surface as it enters Bonne Bay Pond.

 **BROOK ENTRANCE:** N 49.361016, W 57.533727

The trailhead (N 49.351831, W 57.542783) is located off Route 430. The trail to the underground river's entrance is a dirt road that is drivable using an off-road vehicle. Otherwise, the brook's entrance (N 49.361016, W 57.533727) is just a 1.3-kilometre hike along the road. The exit to the river, alongside Route 430 (N 49.356466, W 57.545260), is best seen during high runoff.

CANAL POND-INDIAN DOCK POND CAVE SYSTEM

This is a hidden gem. In the hills above Indian Dock Pond is an unexplored cave system that was carved by a small river travelling between Canal Pond and Indian Dock Pond. Approximately 16 kilometres west of Deer Lake, on a dirt road known as Incinerator Road, the river discharges into Indian Dock Pond. The river, at first sight, seems like any other, but as you walk alongside the riverbed, the amount of water gets smaller and smaller. It is not long before the river disappears altogether, and you are walking in a dried-up riverbed. A little farther up, the riverbed ends abruptly at the face of a steep hill. The end is signified by a landslide that appears to have blocked off the river's exit. If you stand next to the large boulders on a warm, humid day, you feel cool, moist air pushing through the rocks, which is a sign of an air-filled cavern on the other side.

Hiking over the clear-cut mountain, you arrive at a small river flowing north out of Canal Pond. It flows through a small valley before ending abruptly at a debris-covered opening at the edge of a cliff. The water can be heard dropping some distance once it enters the passageway, but without a clear entrance, little can be known about where the water goes.

Another entrance exists nearby. Following the base of the cliff in the direction the river appears to flow, a collapsed roof in the cave (i.e., a sinkhole) provides open access to the cave system. The unpredictable and unexplored cave system is dangerous but observing from the surface provides a worthwhile glimpse inside.

◎ CAVE SYSTEM ENTRANCE: N 49.196128, W 57.672861

The cave system is located between Indian Dock Pond and Canal Pond approximately 14 kilometres west of Deer Lake. An off-road vehicle is essential. The exit to the underground river (N 49.200258, W 57.662072) lies adjacent to Indian Dock Pond, while the entrance to the system (N 49.196128, W 57.672861) involves a short, backcountry hike over the mountains to the south.

6. Corner Brook Stream Caves

Corner Brook, Bay of Islands

Located on the outskirts of Corner Brook is a series of caves carved into the limestone gorge of the Corner Brook Stream. The 400-million-year-old caves make for a great stop for anyone travelling through the area, especially during fall and winter. Today, the easily accessible area is a staple of west coast tourism, and hidden among the birch and spruce forest are many wonders, including sinkholes, stalactites, and, in the winter, ice features. The caves are extremely dangerous to enter, but the best parts of the caves can be seen safely from outside.

HOW DID THE CAVES FORM?

The formation of the Corner Brook Caves began in the Ordovician period, between 488 to 443 million years ago. Early in this period, calcium carbonate sediment was deposited by small organisms located at the bottom of an ancient sea. Over time, the layers of sediment compacted, creating a thick layer of carbonate rock called limestones and dolomites.

This rock layer underwent many changes through the processes of plate tectonics. Approximately 10,000 years ago, fractures in the surrounding rock layers allowed water flowing in the Corner Brook Stream to reach the weak limestone layer. Erosion of the limestone began to occur through a process known as dissolution, where water running over the rock's surface slowly dissolves the rock and carries it downstream. After this process continued for many years, the Corner Brook caves formed.

Today about 450 metres of underground passages remain, dropping in elevation by about 34 metres. In a study done by Richard Chislett, the cave was divided into four sections: the upper section, the depression, the lower section, and the dry entrance. The upper section is that section farthest upstream and is the first to be seen when entering the area.

The next is the depression, a sinkhole where the roof of the cave became too thin to support its own weight, and collapsed. After this, the water dips beneath the surface again through ground-level cracks and flows around a 90-degree bend before exiting back into the Corner Brook Stream.

Midway through the lower section is a dry entrance (no water exists in this portion) about 7 to 8 metres long that connects with the main water channel underground.

Throughout the cave system are several waterfalls, dry passages where water no longer flows, and "rooms" or hollowed-out sections that measure up to 10 metres by 11 metres. Limestone is known for forming features such as potholes, inundations, and ripples, which can be seen on the walls and ceilings, and where you will also see stalactites and stalagmites.

ABOUT THE AREA

While the caves have great tourism potential, they have not been developed due to their inherent danger. Dangerous and unpredictable waterfalls exist inside the entire cave system. Underwater currents pull water down through deep narrow cracks and high ceilings, and sudden drops in the cave floor mean that without the proper knowledge and cave exploration experience, it is too risky. Another source of risk is the weak, and unstable, rock that comprises the caves: it results in collapse and falling rocks.

The greatest risk is the possibility of rapidly changing water levels. Just upstream of the caves is the Three Mile Dam, where water flow is halted and redirected through a penstock to a generation station near Margaret Bowater Park. Signs throughout the area warn of quick and unpredictable water level changes due to the possibility of the dam's spillway opening. Anyone wishing a closer look at the caves should contact Corner Brook Pulp and Paper for water-level information.

Although the caves remain a spectacular place to visit, they can also be extremely dangerous. Several tour operators have provided tours of the caves in the past, the most recent by Cycles Solutions on West Street. Only enter the caves with an experienced guide.

 **CORNER BROOK STREAM CAVES:** N 48.924842, W 57.903203

These caves are located on the upper section of the Corner Brook stream, northwest of Three Mile Dam.

Westbound from Corner Brook on the Trans-Canada Highway from the Exit 5 (Massey Drive) overpass, travel approximately 1.25 kilometres and turn right onto a small unpaved road where the trailhead is located (N 48.926593, W 57.902515). Park beside the road. Hike approximately 300 metres: the entrance is along the river. Other points of interest such as the sinkhole (N 48.925565, W 57.904563) and exit (N 48.927246, W 57.903660) are nearby. Other entrances to the caves can be found along the river and in the surrounding forest.

7. Valmont Drive-In

Irishtown-Summerside, Bay of Islands

Peeking out of the forest near the community of Irishtown-Summerside is a large rectangular structure that was once an enormous screen belonging to the Valmont Drive-In Theatre. The drive-in, operational from the mid-1970s to -1980s, built by Jack O'Brien, a local businessperson from Curling, was owned and operated by Willis French.

The Valmont Drive-In has little recorded history. Most of this information was recounted by people who lived in the area. Little remains of the drive-in theatre today except for the large concrete foundation for the projector house, concession stand, and theatre screen. It provides a glimpse of the enormous screens used in this once-favourite type of entertainment.

⊕ **VALMONT DRIVE-IN:** N 49.000962, W 57.895421
The road to the drive-in is located approximately 100 metres west of Hughes Brook Bridge on Route 440. Drive (or walk) along the trail for 300 metres and turn left for the site. The large screen is hard to miss, even from the main road.

8. York Harbour Mine
York Harbour, Bay of Islands

High on the Blow Me Down Mountains near the community of York Harbour is an abandoned copper mine. Remnants of this once-prosperous industry—mine shafts, carts, drainage systems, and equipment—litter the landscape. The mine goes unnoticed by most; however, it has prominently affected the landscape.

HISTORY

The story of the York Harbour Mine begins in 1893 with the discovery of a copper deposit approximately 300 metres up a narrow river valley on the Blow Me Down Mountains. Founder Daniel Henderson spent four years attempting to gather funds to finance the mining operation before eventually finding success with St. John's merchant A.J. Harvey. This led to the official start of the mine in 1897. Four poorly planned mine shafts were dug and a series of substandard chutes, pulley systems, and ore transport systems were constructed. Little ore was extracted and, with the mine's uncertain future, the manager was fired and the copper deposit leased to the York Harbour Copper Company based out of England.

The mine slowly progressed. The four mineshafts were deepened and some of the equipment was upgraded. However, by 1902 only 100 tons of ore had been extracted. Plagued by a fire that forced a brief evacuation of the mine, conflicts with French Navy vessels (land was at the time still under the ownership of France), and a dysentery outbreak in nearby communities, the owners allowed the lease to the mineral deposit to expire.

In 1902, the mine came under the ownership of the Humber Consolidated Mining and Manufacturing Company. With high expectations, the underground workings were expanded, an underground railroad constructed, and a complex ore transportation system consisting of tramways and chutes was developed to transport the ore to a loading facility near the water. About 15,000 tons of ore were extracted between 1902 and 1905. But once again, the company encountered financial and management problems, and the mine was turned over to the Western Copper Company in 1906, and then to the York Harbour Mine (Newfoundland) Ltd. in 1909. The mine faced constant labour shortages and, after the collapse of several levels of the mine, one of which reportedly killed a miner, the mine was shut down. The last load of ore departed York Harbour in 1913.

The mine remained dormant until the second half of the 20th century, when a series of drilling and explorative mining operations were completed every two to five years until the late 2010s.

ABOUT THE AREA

After the mine closed in 1913, the wooden barracks and mining buildings were abandoned and left to decay. Today pieces of these buildings are visible alongside the ore transport and water systems. While much of the equipment was removed by locals over time, throughout the forest—confined by the steep sides of the gorge the mine sits in—are boilers, steel equipment, and multiple large mining carts. The mine shafts have either collapsed or been buried by the eroding sides of the valley.

The last remaining sign of a physical mine in the area is the partially blocked opening of an adit (horizontal shaft) near the parking lot of the Copper Mine Falls Trail and Cape Blow Me Down Trail. This explorative mine, dug in 1965 by the company Big Nama, travels 800 metres into the hillside. A fire in 1966 caused major damage to the buildings and thus halted the operation.

The York Harbour mine was a hopeful endeavour plagued by troubles. Today the area offers the excitement of exploring a 120-year-old mine site, and its location atop the Blow Me Down Mountains offers spectacular vistas.

YORK HARBOR MINE: N 49.049603, W 58.308712

The trailhead (N 49.061983, W 58.309942) is approximately 550 metres west of the Cape Blow Me Down parking lot. The ATV trail is fairly regularly used; although the trail is in good condition, it is steep in certain sections. The first mine site is located 1.2 kilometres up the trail; the second, 1.6 kilometres. Be sure to check out the adit entrance, which can be viewed in the Cape Blow Me Down parking lot.

9. Cedar Cove

Little Port, Bay of Islands

Cedar Cove, Wild Cove, and Capelin Cove are all names given to the small indent of coastline near the opening of the Bay of Islands. But whatever you wish to call it, Cedar Cove is worth a visit. The charming little cove is home to a small rocky beach sandwiched between the hills of the Blow Me Down Mountains.

Cedar Cove is the perfect place to visit for a quick, off-the-beaten-path picnic spot while travelling through the Bay of Islands.

CEDAR COVE: N 49.090808, W 58.423214

A flat, well-maintained 1.8-kilometre-long trail leaves from the small community of Little Port and provides easy access to the cove.

10. Governor's Staircase

Lark Harbour, Bay of Islands

There are staircases and then there is the Governor's Staircase in Blow Me Down Provincial Park. Tucked away in the hills of the Bay of Islands, this unique staircase is constructed inside an eroded limestone cave. A small stream flowing down the hillside eroded the 450-million-year-old limestone, creating the natural overhang in which the stairs were built. The staircase also marks the start of a short hike to the top of the mountain, where an observation platform provides a 360-degree view of the Bay of Islands.

GOVERNOR'S STAIRCASE: N 49.090258, W 58.362251

The staircase is easily accessed in Blow Me Down Provincial Park (in Lark Harbour) by walking west along the park's south beach. The staircase is well marked, and assistance is available at the park's entrance booth.

11. Bottle Cove Sea Cave

Bottle Cove, Lark Harbour

Sea caves, usually found along cliffsides, are often extremely difficult to get to and require a combination of calm seas, low tide, and convenient access points. The sea cave found on the exposed cliffs outside Bottle Cove is no different. The large cave carved into the dark, basaltic rocks is difficult to access except during extremely low tides—but it is not as difficult to see.

Following the trails to Bottle Cove's scenic sunset rocks and the dark and jagged rocks that make up the cove's shoreline provides a panoramic vantage point. Bottle Cove itself is a hidden gem. The grass-lined hills along the shores of the perfectly round bay are protected by the towering mountains. The grassy headland at the northern side of the narrow passage into the cove contrasts with the dark rocks of the cliff faces. These dark rocks are primarily made from the geologic feature pillow lava, formed by lava that rises above the sea floor before quickly hardening and forming the distinctive pillow-shaped mounds. Several well-maintained trails lead along the seaside and share the area's history.

⊕ BOTTLE COVE SEA CAVE: N 49.113474, W 58.412426

From Lark Harbour, follow Little Port Road for 2.2 kilometres and turn onto Beacon Road. Drive a short distance on the gravel road to a parking lot and the trailhead (N 49.117178, W 58.406151). Follow the signs to the grassy headland about 500 metres away. The cave can be seen across the cove's narrow opening.

12. Copper Mine Falls
York Harbour

Gaining its name from the successful mining operation on the banks of the river over 120 years ago, Copper Mine Falls is located just 300 metres from the main south shore highway (Route 450). The river originates from the mountaintop of Cape Blow Me Down. After flowing through one of the many narrow gullies winding through the forested hill, the falls drop 20 metres onto the rocks below. The waterfall's easy access, short distance from the main road, and scenery will not disappoint.

COPPER MINE FALLS: N 49.059510, W 58.304802

The trailhead (N 49.061773, W 58.304979) is located at the start of the Cape Blow Me Down Mountain hiking trail. Park in the designated parking lot and follow the trail at the far end of the lot for about 300 metres to the base of the falls. Do not hike up the stairs unless you are prepared: this strenuous trail leads to the Cape Blow Me Down mountain summit.

13. Swimming Hole atop Steady Brook Falls

Steady Brook

Overlooking the community of Steady Brook is one of the west coast's most impressive waterfalls. Steady Brook Falls cascades over the east side of Marble Mountain into a narrow gorge before flowing into the Humber River. The waterfall, approximately 50 metres high, is best viewed from a community-maintained hiking trail and lookout. Each year many locals venture to a deep pool at the top of the falls—a popular swimming hole for those willing to risk the currents and frigid water.

The trail to the swimming hole is challenging. This slippery trail descends into the river gorge, where a steep drop must be navigated before arriving at the swimming hole. At one end, the river falls through a narrow rock cut before flowing into the pool. At the other, the pool becomes shallow as it rises over the side and immediately falls over what might as well be the edge of the world. This unsupervised swimming location is dangerous but hundreds of people make the trek each year.

◎ **SWIMMING HOLE:** N 48.947226, W 57.822365

To access the trailhead to the falls, turn onto Thistle Drive, just behind George's Ski World. Before crossing the bridge into Marble Wood, turn right into the gravel parking area. Park at the base of the hill. On foot, follow the community trail signs to the waterfall's main lookout, approximately 500 metres up the hill. The swimming location is located farther along the trail near the top of the falls.

14. Corner Brook Quarry Falls

Corner Brook

Hidden among the many waterfalls and brooks that wind through the town of Corner Brook is Corner Brook Quarry Falls, found along an unnamed brook flowing out of the large limestone quarry in Corner Brook's east end. This site resembles terraced waterfalls seen elsewhere in the world, usually formed by hot springs dissolving limestone and producing terraced pools interlaced with small waterfalls. But while these waterfalls display the same small, terraced pooling found in hot springs around the world, the origin of these falls is far from natural.

The limestone quarry that the brook flows through has been in operation since North Star Cement began excavating the hillside in 1952 for materials for its nearby cement plant. At one time, this plant produced 90 per cent of the cement used on the island of Newfoundland. The cement plant continued mining the quarry until its closure in 2000; afterward, it was maintained as a slate and rock quarry. But the long history of cement production had its downside, mainly in the form of excess cement and slag, the fine-grained waste material that likely created the waterfall that exists today. Over the years, improper disposal of this carbonate-rich material led to its being washed downstream, where the carbonates settled and moulded together to create the falls.

The brook transports this material farther downstream, forming small ripples, terraced pools, and icelike filaments. The small waterfall and its fragile terraces look to be straight out of an alien world. In reality, this site is a reminder of past industries and their unnatural effects on the local environment.

 **CORNER BROOK QUARRY FALLS:** N 48.953187, W 57.898363

This waterfall occurs along a local snowmobile/ATV trail. Because the quarry is still in operation, the only access to the falls is from the trailhead near Tippings Pond in Massey Drive. Follow the unmaintained trail for approximately 1.1 kilometres, then turn left onto the snowmobile trail and hike another 3.2 kilometres. The brook and waterfall intersect the trail and is best seen alongside it.

Lark Harbour
Corner Brook
11
5 Fox Island River
Lourdes
9
8 6 4 2
Mainland
7 3 1
12
10
Stephenville
Cape St. George
Flat Bay
Bay St. George South
13
Great Codroy
14
Cape Ray
15
Rose Blanche-Harbour le Cou
Burgeo
Channel-Port aux Basques
Isle aux Morts

Southwest Coast

Port au Port Peninsula, St. George's Bay, & Southwest Coast

Crystal-clear Caribbean blue waters; twisting coastal roads; high, flat-topped mountains; and lush green estuaries are just a few of the highlights of this area. From the southern terminus of Lewis Hills to historic Rose Blanche in the south, this region encompasses numerous geographies and cultures. Located on a low-lying terrace at the north end of St. George's Bay is the town of Stephenville. Founded by the United States Air Force, the town has an American-style layout that makes it like no other place in Newfoundland. Nearby, the Port au Port Peninsula offers one of the most scenic drives on the island. On the south coast, the Table Mountains and Long Range Mountains rise above Channel-Port aux Basques—the first view for visitors arriving on the ferry from Nova Scotia … if the weather co-operates. Known for treacherous seas and dense fog, the rocky coastline of the south shore is the beautiful, rugged scenery for which Newfoundland is best known. Behind the mountains, though, the Codroy Valley reflects the grassy, lush estuaries and farmland of Nova Scotia.

The story of the south coast begins with the use of the sandy beach-lined Codroy Valley and St. George's Bay by the Mi'kmaq of Nova Scotia. The Mi'kmaq fished and hunted along this water before permanent European settlers arrived, centuries later. The area was then used mainly by French fishers, whose legacy is still found in the many French-influenced names in the area. In the early 19th century, the fishery attracted many English, who settled in places such as Rose Blanche for its proximity to the Grand Bank fishing grounds.

The construction of the Newfoundland Railway at the end of the 19th century brought great change to the area. Better access meant more people and more industry. In the Codroy Valley, the farms that were created were some of the first and most productive agricultural lands anywhere in the province. In the Port au Port Peninsula and Stephenville areas, new mines were established, which are still visible in the towns of St. George's, Sheaves Cove, and Aguathuna. Perhaps nothing affected the area more than the choice of Stephenville, once a small fishing community, as home to an American Air Force Base during World War II and the Cold

War. This improved infrastructure and transportation networks drastically changed the culture of the town. After the base closed, the economic boom subsided, but the area is sustained by resource-based industries such as agriculture, fishing, and mining.

The towns of Stephenville and Stephenville Crossing are located along Route 460. Continuing west to the Port au Port Peninsula, Route 463 loops around the peninsula. Following the Trans-Canada Highway south, Routes 403, 404, and 405 lead to the communities of Flat Bay, Robinsons, and Saint David's. These coastal fishing and farming communities offer spectacular scenery, beaches, and views of the several large rivers that flow from the mountains to St. George's Bay. Continuing farther south on the Trans-Canada Highway, Routes 406 and 407 branch off to twist through the Codroy Valley before the main highway continues to the Port aux Basques ferry terminal. Be sure to continue and explore Route 470 to Rose Blanche for a glimpse of the rugged south coast.

1. Ernest Harmon Air Force Base
Stephenville, West Coast

In 1940 the Destroyers for Bases Agreement was signed by the United Kingdom and the United States, granting the US 99-year land leases in any British colony. This crucial document resulted in significant changes to Newfoundland; nowhere is this better demonstrated than in Stephenville.

The community's wartime boom extended into the Cold War; the base was decommissioned, and the land turned over to local governments in 1966. Today the area is scarred with wartime remnants: bunkers, tunnels, buildings, and the airfield itself. Many of these structures have been repurposed; others have been abandoned or dismantled. Embedded in these remnants are stories and mysteries, all of which make Stephenville a fascinating place.

HISTORY

Prior to 1940, Stephenville was the small fishing village of Acadian Village, a name which originated from the large population of Acadian families who had immigrated there from Cape Breton.

After the signing of the Destroyers for Bases Agreement on September 2, 1940, the US selected several sites in Newfoundland for military defence bases, including Stephenville. Just four months after the signing of the agreement, engineering troops and civilian specialists began surveying the area in preparation for the construction of an airfield. The following month, 150 members of the US Signal Corps began setting up temporary housing to be used during the construction of the base. Also joining them was the 24th Coastal Artillery group, whose duty was to set up

protection for the base. Construction also began on a deepwater port near the airfield site to deliver supplies and materials.

The primary purpose of the Stephenville Air Base was to be a stopover and refuelling point for military aircraft crossing the Atlantic. Upon completion, this base was the largest US military airfield outside the continental US.

During the construction of the base, the neighbouring small village of Stephenville began to expand as well. Dozens of new buildings were constructed, and a mass influx of military personnel resulted in a huge economic boom to the region.

After the war had ended, the airfield continued to be used as a primary refuelling point for military aircraft, and on June 23,

1948, the base itself was renamed Ernest Harmon Air Force Base in honour of Captain Ernest Emery Harmon, an Army Air Corps pilot who was killed in an air crash in 1933. The deepwater port nearby was given the name Port Harmon.

In 1950, the airfield was transferred to the Northeast Air Command, and in April 1957 to the Strategic Air Command (SAC). The Cold War was just beginning and the threat of attack by the Soviet Union was high. As a refuelling point, Harmon hosted a fleet of KC-97 Stratofreighters, which were used to refuel nuclear armed B-52 Stratofortress aircraft that were constantly in the air on high alert in case of an attack. A squadron of F-102 Flight Interceptor aircraft was also stationed at the base.

During the Cold War, many upgrades were completed on the base. In 1953, the 347th Engineer Aviation Battalion constructed 186,000 square metres of runways, 352,000 square metres of taxiways and tarmac, as well as aircraft hangers and a control tower, and upgraded docking facilities at Port Harmon. Much of the base that is seen today was constructed at this time, including many of the buildings, housing, and even the Hansen Memorial Highway, which was built to prevent civilians from having to drive through the base. During this time, Harmon was selected as one of the few sites in Canada equipped to store nuclear weapons; further upgrades and security were added to accommodate this.

As Cold War tensions dissipated and technology advanced, the need for a large military facility in Stephenville declined, and on December 16, 1966, the base was decommissioned. Although its the lease was for 99 years, after its closure the property was transferred to the Government of Canada and subsequently to the Government of Newfoundland and Labrador.

The Harmon Corporation was established to oversee the re-purposing and redeveloping of the newly acquired land. Part of this was the development of the Stephenville International Airport, which uses a portion of the original air force base.

ABOUT THE AREA

Airfield Hangers & Facilities

Along the older sections of the airfield, many of the original aircraft hangars are still being used for industrial and commercial storage. During World War II and the Cold War, these hangers hosted some of the world's largest military aircraft.

One building sure to capture the attention of people passing

by is the "Mole Hole." The one-storey building has several tunnels protruding out of each side with many dipping below the ground. The building has been the epicentre of many stories and myths involving secret underground tunnels and bunkers. But the true purpose of the subsurface building was to house the aircraft crews that were on constant alert in case of an attack. The underground housing was designed to withstand a near-miss of a nuclear weapon and allow the occupants to quickly get to their aircraft in preparation for a counterstrike. Today it continues to be used as a storage facility (N 48.553821, W 58.543740).

Bunkers

Harmon also contained many ammunition and explosives bunkers. Most are dome-shaped, concrete bunkers covered by earth and shrubs on three sides, with a steel door on the fourth. Commonly called "igloos," these damp underground rooms are up to 18 metres long and 8 metres wide, with the highest point of the arched roof reaching almost 4 metres.

These bunkers are scattered throughout Stephenville, but the largest clusters are located on a golf course near Port Harmon just north of the town on the appropriately named Igloo Road. Many are still used for residential and commercial storage (N 48.563309, W 58.556618).

Special Weapons Storage Bunker

Tucked away in the hills, far from the airbase, is a large building resembling a modern storage unit. The difference between them is the thick reinforced concrete walls and large, heavy steel doors protecting each of the small rectangular rooms. This building is one of the base's special weapons storage bunkers that housed critical ammunition and explosives. The building's distant location was to prevent it from being damaged or destroyed in the event of enemy attack (N 48.542184, W 58.501627).

Crematorium

Located behind the modern hospital, the two-storey crematorium is distinguishable by its large chimney marked with four crosses. The building, inaccessible due to its deteriorated condition, has been the basis of numerous ghost stories (N 48.559141, W 58.549372).

Tank Farm

Watch for the numerous fuel tanks in the hills surrounding the base, the remains of the large fuel storage system that once supplied the base. The tanks were spaced out so that, in the event of an attack, the entire system would not be taken out.

⊕ **AIR FORCE BASE:** N 48.551881, W 58.545544

The base is comprised of what is today the east side of Stephenville, a town located approximately 28 kilometres west of the Trans-Canada Highway along Route 460.

2. Blanche Brook

Stephenville

Entering the western side of Stephenville on the Hansen Memorial Highway (Route 460), you pass over a small river named Blanche Brook. What is not obvious at first is the brook's notable geologic significance. Scattered throughout the smooth riverbed are the fossils of 305-million-year-old trees. These fossilized logs represent the earliest known seed-producing trees to grow on the thin soils of mountain slopes. The rocks making up the area were located on the supercontinent of Pangea 305 million years ago, farther south than their location today. These tropical trees grew over 50 metres tall. The trunks of the Blanche Brook trees were filled with dark grey sediment, preserving them and providing a clear contrast against the light-coloured sandstone of the riverbed.

The fossils were first recorded in an 1873 report by the Newfoundland Geological Survey. In the past several years, however, recognition of the fossil site has resulted in the creation of a trail system that follows the river and provides easy access to it. If you are passing through the town of Stephenville, it is worth the short hike to find the fossils scattered through the normally shallow river.

BLANCHE BROOK FOSSILS: N 48.566662, W 58.586288 Travelling along the Hansen Memorial Highway (Route 460), turn onto Riverside Drive located next to MF Motorsports and Route 460 Powersports. The parking lot and trailhead are located on the left side of the road. From there, a 500-metre-long, well-maintained trail leads to the fossil site.

3. Gypsum Cliffs & a Sinkhole Forest
Romaines Brook, Kippens

As you drive along Route 460 toward the Port au Port Peninsula, you descend into the Romaines Brook river valley. Heading west toward the Port au Port it is easy to overlook the white cliffs on the eastern riverbanks, but on the return trip, the bright white pinnacles embedded on the side of the forested riverbank are impossible to miss. This geologic wonder is made of gypsum which has become exposed by the river and sculpted to its unique shape by rain and snow.

This gypsum formed almost 360 million years ago during the Carboniferous period, when the area was a shallow sea. Over time, the sea evaporated, leaving behind sediment, or evaporates, which is generally salt or gypsum. The weak, easily erodible rock was preserved underground for most of its history until plate tectonics forced it above ground. Eventually, the nearby river eroded the ground and exposed the cliffs that are visible today.

The mineral potential of the gypsum was recognized in the 1890s when Charles Osman extracted the ore and sold it to markets in Canada and the US. After the site was abandoned due to France's land rights along what was then the French Shore, the rock was not mined again until 1926, when the Reid Newfoundland Company dug several tunnels and test pits into the hillside. Today, all evidence of these expeditions is gone, but it is estimated that over 2 million tons of gypsum remain in the hillside.

Gypsum-like carbonate minerals erode quicker than other rocks and produce karst landforms, which are typically the base rocks that form caves, sinkholes, and other strange-looking formations. The rocks here are no different. The forest behind the cliffs is a chaotic landscape where dozens of deep sinkholes and pits have dramatically changed the forest floor. This is the result of years of underground and surface erosion.

Exercise caution, as the rocks are very unstable and walking along them accelerates erosion. From the main highway and a nearby dirt road, the cliffs can be safely appreciated and preserved.

GYPSUM CLIFFS: N 48.553140, W 58.671172

The cliffs are located on the east side of Romaines Brook, approximately 5.8 kilometres west of Stephenville. From Route 460 and Brennan Lane, a gravel road located on the west side of the river, the cliffs tower through the forest across the river.

4. Western Pinetree Line Radar Station

Port au Port East

Shortly after World War II, the Cold War was in full force. Out of fear of invasion, the United States Air Force (with aid from the Royal Canadian Air Force) built several radar stations approximately along the 50th parallel, known as the Pinetree Line. These stations would track all aircraft travelling across North America and act as an early warning system.

One radar station was built on a hilltop near the community of Kippens overlooking the Port au Port Peninsula and the Gulf of St. Lawrence. Today, several abandoned buildings, piles of scrap metal, and pieces of equipment are all that remain of this station. Anyone willing to hike to the old station will be rewarded with spectacular scenery.

HISTORY

The radar site, located on top of Table Mountain near the community of Kippens, approximately 7.5 kilometres west of Stephenville, was officially classified as a general surveillance radar station that would detect unidentified aircraft's altitude, speed, and direction, which it could then relay to intercept fighter jets located at the nearby Harmon Air Force Base.

The site was built in 1952 by the United States Air Force and at the time placed under the command of the Air National Guard. The following year the radar station changed ownership, this time under the control of the 640th Aircraft Control and Warning Squadron, where it operated as a Pinetree Line site.

Similar to many other Cold War-era radar sites, this complex was completely self-supported and self-contained: it supplied its own power, provided its own water, and contained living accommodations for all personnel. It also contained several large operations and support buildings, the foundations of which are visible today.

The site operated for almost a decade, but advancements in radar and early warning systems made the station obsolete. In 1971, it was decommissioned and most of the equipment and buildings were removed. Although the radar station was never used for its intended purpose, it aided in many rescue operations and in the navigation of aircraft travelling over the Gulf of St. Lawrence.

ABOUT THE AREA

Not everything was removed from the base. A small concrete building, piles of scrap metal, and the foundations of the original radar and operations building are still visible today. The one remaining radar dome is being used by the communication towers and Coast Guard facilities on the mountain.

The steel structure of one of the site's radar domes was dismantled during the construction of the Pine Tree Ski Resort located lower on the hill, and used as the primary structure for the ski lodge, which can still be seen.

Numerous communication towers are still active on the site and the road to it is well maintained. Hiking the road and hills surrounding the old radar complex is worthwhile for the views of St. George's Bay and the Port au Port Peninsula.

When hiking the mountain, look for a small plant known as the Low Northern Rockcress, an endangered plant species found exclusively among the low shrubs of Table Mountain.

RADAR STATION: N 48.590288, W 58.666416

After travelling to Port au Port East, turn north onto Hynes Road (Route 462) toward Fox Island River. Approximately 2.7 kilometres in, a dirt road on the right offers parking space. Hiking on the dirt road (Pine Tree Road) for 4 kilometres brings you to the top of the mountain to the radar site.

Caution
Electric
Fence

5. Fox Island Lighthouse

Fox Island River, Port au Port Bay

As you drive along Route 462 between Kippens and Fox Island River, you notice a strange sight. Peeking out of the treetops, almost 130 metres from the shoreline, is the top of a lighthouse. And while the sight is unusual, so are the circumstances that put it there.

The lighthouse was built almost 8 kilometres north of this location in 1955. It was built 300 metres from another lighthouse and together the two battery-powered towers created a navigational tool known as a light range, at Broad Cove Point. The 5.2-metre-high tower replaced an older lighthouse that was built there in 1909 to mark the eastern extremity of the Port au Port Bay.

In 2005, after 60 years of service, the lights were decommissioned by the Coast Guard. A resident from nearby Fox Island River purchased the top of the lighthouse to serve as a well cover. But upon picking up the piece, the new owner decided to accept the Coast Guard's offer to take the rest of the lighthouse. With the help of a Coast Guard helicopter, the lighthouse was airlifted in multiple pieces to the backyard of the new owner's house.

The new owner restored the lighthouse, even using parts and materials from the other lighthouse at Broad Cove Point. It now stands proudly above the treetops, with its light shining once again.

FOX ISLAND LIGHTHOUSE: N 48.688082, W 58.683674

Heading toward Port au Port, turn left onto Hynes Road (Route 462) and drive about 17 kilometres. The lighthouse is approximately 100 metres in, on the right side of the road. Permission from the landowner is required to get any closer to it.

6. The Gravels Walking Trail

Port au Port West-Aguathuna-Felix Cove

Driving to the Port au Port Peninsula, you cross a narrow isthmus that connects the peninsula to the main island. The isthmus consists of two back-to-back beaches known as The Gravels. As you approach the far side of the isthmus, a parking lot marks the beginning of a walking trail that brings you through some of the peninsula's coastal rocks and limestone formations. Recently renamed Danny's Trail, this easy-to-walk coastal trail passes low limestone cliffs that have been carved into unique and strange formations. Dome-shaped rocks, rows of sea stacks, and perfectly rounded columns of rock seemingly balancing on the edge of cliffs are must-see features of the trail.

The limestone rocks were deposited in a shallow ocean reef during the Mississippian period, about 330 million years ago. As a result, along the cliffs and rocks that the trail follows are numerous fossils of ancient underwater creatures. Many resemble shells permanently embedded in the rock—spend some time searching for signs of coral and trilobite-like creatures. Be sure to leave the area as you found it: as with any area containing fossils, it is illegal to remove fossils from this location.

ROCK FORMATIONS: N 48.561194, W 58.734515

The trailhead (N 48.558571, W 58.730105) is located about 12 kilometres west of Stephenville on Route 460 toward the Port au Port Peninsula. Walk along the leisurely, well-maintained trail for approximately 500 metres to the first rock formation and fossils.

7. Lead Cove Mine

Port au Port West-Aguathuna-Felix Cove

Along the coastal trail now known as Danny's Trail is a small, rocky beach located in the aptly named Lead Cove. Lead had been noticed near the cove since the early 20th century while prospecting was being completed for the Aguathuna Limestone Quarry located nearby. Little interest was taken in the lead until the 1970s, when an exploration mine was excavated into the hillside to investigate the rocks' mineral potential. The mine only went into the hillside a short distance before it was determined that the lead content was not viable for mining. The endeavour and the mine were abandoned.

The entrance to the mine is located behind the cove's rocky beach. For those who do not know the story, the mine could easily be mistaken for a sea cave. Entering the mine is not recommended. Signs of collapse can be seen on the cave floor from the entrance, and the weak rock that the area is known for is unstable.

⊕ **LEAD COVE MINE:** N 48.559979, W 58.741575

The trailhead (N 48.558571, W 58.730105) is located approximately 12 kilometres west of Stephenville on Route 460 toward the Port au Port Peninsula. From here, Lead Cove is a 1-kilometre-long hike along the well-maintained trail.

A shorter route is possible from a trailhead (N 48.558463, W 58.740892) located along Main Street in Aguathuna. Park along the road; a 175-metre-long trail brings you to the cove.

8. Aguathuna Limestone Quarry

Aguathuna, Port au Port Peninsula

Little remains of the Aguathuna Limestone Quarry located on the eastern edge of the Port au Port Peninsula. The scarred landscape was once home to a critical mine that supplied the Cape Breton Steel Mills with limestone used in the extraction of iron ore from the Bell Island Mine on the east coast. In addition to the strange light-coloured plateau, some remnants of this mine still exist, including building foundations, large conveyor belts, and underground tunnels.

But the limestone that made the mine so productive also created a landscape that is not commonly experienced in Newfoundland and Labrador. The ocean's erosion of the weak limestone rock formed caves, sea stacks, and rock formations. The gradual breakdown of limestone produces another unique trait: crystal clear waters created from the introduction of calcium carbonate

(the chemical compound that makes up limestone rock). The waters are comparable in appearance to the clear waters found in the Caribbean Sea.

HISTORY

The quarry was opened in 1911 by the Dominion Iron and Steel Company (also referred to as the Nova Scotia Iron and Steel Company) from Sydney, Nova Scotia. When iron ore mining began on Bell Island in the early 20th century by the same company, limestone was needed in the process of purifying and separating the iron from its parent rock.

In addition to vast quantities of limestone deposits located on the surface, Aguathuna was also chosen because of its proximity to the Port au Port Bay and to the steel mines themselves. Jack of Clubs Cove was renamed Aguathuna by the quarry's manager, Arthur House, who believed Aguathuna to be the Beothuk word for "white stone." The name, however, actually translated to "Grindstone."

The mine was open seasonally and originally used a 2,600-pound steel ball to excavate the soft rock instead of traditional methods such as explosives. After the rock was loosened, it was placed on carts drawn by horses, transported to a large wharf, and loaded onto cargo ships.

In the 1920s, steam-powered shovels guided by a series of tracks replaced the steel ball, and small locomotives and conveyor belt systems replaced horses and carts. Around this time, the mine reached its peak productivity, employing about 500 area residents.

The Aguathuna Quarry operated until 1964, when it closed due to financial difficulties and the discovery of deposits closer to the processing plants in Cape Breton. During its operation, the mine was a critical industry; its closure was a significant loss to the area.

ABOUT THE LOCATION

Limestone cliffs line the quarry along the southern reach of Port au Port Bay. As the road winds down into the quarry, signs of the mining operation appear. A barren rock terrace and deteriorating concrete foundations are the remaining signs of the operation visible from the road. Farther along the coast are remnants of the loading dock, buildings, conveyor belt systems, and equipment.

As with most of the south coast of the bay, exploring the coastline reveals a carved limestone landscape that consists of sea stacks, caves, arches, and crystal-clear waters. Back near the road, a two-storey concrete building seems to fit with the abandoned quarry. But don't be fooled: this is an operational training building for local firefighters.

The mine is relatively safe, as no underground mining was done. It is also located immediately adjacent to a provincial highway, making it easy to access. A small quarry continues to operate nearby; do not trespass or interfere with the operation.

◎ LIMESTONE QUARRY: N 48.561544, W 58.772021
As you enter the Port au Port Peninsula via The Gravels, continue straight (do not follow Route 460 left) on Main Street for approximately 1.7 kilometres. Turn right, stay on Main Street for another 1.8 kilometres to arrive at the quarry.

9. West Bay & Jerry's Nose Transmitter Sites

Port au Port Peninsula

The facilities to support Harmon Air Force Base in Stephenville spread not only through the town but also to most of the region. This is perhaps best seen on the Port au Port Peninsula, where in 1952 the United States acquired two land lots to construct large communication and radar sites in the communities of West Bay and Jerry's Nose. These satellite sites, constructed in 1953, were operated by the 1933d Communications Squadron that was part of the United States Air Force Airways and Air Communication Service. The older site at Jerry's Nose began as part of the Pinetree Line System designed to detect aircraft and missiles during the Cold War but was then converted to the sole purpose of a receiver site to pick up signals from the mainland. Its counterpart at West Bay was a transmitter site capable of sending messages to other US bases and nearby aircraft.

The 3-square-kilometre complex at West Bay and 1.5-square-kilometre facility at Jerry's Nose were comprised of many buildings and each contained a complex array of antennas and communications towers. The sites were constructed with the aid of residents and partly operated and maintained by them. This provided small communities with employment opportunities and the takeover of the land by the US government was welcomed.

Not only are these sites a reminder of how far technology has come since the 1950s and 1960s but also how far the US government was willing to go during the Cold War to create these defence networks. In Jerry's Nose, nothing but the vague outline of paths and the odd foundation exists on the headland overlooking St. George's Bay. At the West Bay site, one or two concrete support buildings still mark the outer edge of the site. The four roads that once protruded outward from a central operations building at the complex now access farmland in the area. Because of this, the site is no longer accessible.

 **JERRY'S NOSE SITE:** N 48.516390, W 58.930427

The Jerry's Nose site is located at the end of Site Road, which intersects Route 460 approximately 1 kilometre west of the turnoff to Route 463 in Abrahams Cove.

 **WEST BAY SITE:** N 48.619383, W 58.985478

The West Bay site is located west of Route 463 in the community of West Bay. It can be seen from the road; it is now private property and can no longer be accessed.

10. Kissing Rocks Sea Arch

Jerry's Nose, Port au Port Peninsula

Resembling two people smooching, the one-of-a-kind formation is technically both a sea arch and a sea stack. However you choose to classify it, the formation is the result of thousands of years of waves and sea ice eroding the cliff face. The arch, one of the many geologic wonders of the Port au Port Peninsula, is located at the end of a gravel road in Jerry's Nose.

KISSING ROCKS SEA ARCH: N 48.508282, W 58.941734
The arch is located at the end of Jerry's Nose Road, which intersects Route 460 approximately 1.7 kilometres west of the turnoff to Route 463 in Abrahams Cove. A short walk over gravel terrain is then required to view the arch.

11. Long Point

Port au Port Peninsula

Protruding almost 20 kilometres out into the Gulf of St. Lawrence, Long Point encloses the western side of Port au Port Bay. Also known as "The Bar," Long Point is a narrow peninsula that extends northwest of the Port au Port Peninsula. The peninsula begins with a width of 2.5 kilometres, which decreases to 320 metres before tapering off to a single point, nearly 13 kilometres away. Driving the peninsula offers dramatic views, with water on both sides. After reaching the community of Blue Beach, the

northern extremity is a 2.5-kilometre-long hike over a rocky barren landscape.

◎ **LONG POINT:** N 48.782070, W 58.770880

From the community of Lourdes on Route 463, turn north onto Clam Bank Cove Road (Route 464). Travel approximately 21.5 kilometres on the mostly gravel road to arrive at the cabin community of Blue Beach. From here, a 2.5-kilometre-long hike along a coastal ATV trail brings you to the tip of Long Point.

12. Port au Port Crash

Cape St. George, Port au Port Peninsula

On the night of November 12, 1944, a United States Army Air Force C-54A left LaGuardia airfield for Harmon Air Force Base in Stephenville. Captain E.C. Walkins was an experienced pilot who had checked the weather and route path before taking off. During the flight, however, it is believed that Walkins failed to regularly check his navigation equipment, and an incoming storm pushed the plane off course. Without warning, the low flying plane crashed into a forested hill just north of Cape St. George.

Of the 18 crew members aboard, nine, including Walkins, were killed instantly when the plane hit the ground. As the sun began to rise, the surviving crew launched signal flares and began making their way out of the woods to find help. The crew found a local man, who helped bring them to safety. Around the same time, rescue planes spotted the crash site and immediately sent additional help. This tragic accident was blamed on unpredictable weather and pilot negligence. In the following days, three more crew members perished from their injuries.

Pieces of engine, landing gear, and rusted objects mark the crash site's location, a short walk from the main highway.

◎ **PORT AU PORT CRASH: N 48.494940, W 59.225241**
The trailhead (N 48.494294, W 59.221940) is located approximately 4.4 kilometres north of Cape St. George. Parking is available in a small gravel lot located off the main highway (Route 460/463). A 300-metre-long walk brings you to the site.

13. Highlands Sea Stacks

Highlands

South of the community of Highlands is a series of sea stacks rising above a sandy beach. The coastal terrace ends abruptly, with tall sandy cliffs dropping to the beach below. Over many thousands of years, the terrace has eroded, leaving behind several tall sea stacks and a long sandy beach.

The largest of the sea stacks, located close to the shore, is accessible on foot at low tide. The other, much smaller, stack, home to a small colony of cormorants, is farther out at sea.

The area is complemented by the surrounding mountains and waterfalls. Located at the southern extremity of St. George's Bay, the beach marks the start of the Anguille Mountains, which continue to the Codroy Valley. Although the cliffs are steep and sandy at the beach, farther south they turn to solid rock with multiple waterfalls flowing over them into the ocean.

A lookout lets you view the beach from high up on the hill, while an unmaintained wooden staircase provides access to the beach below. Be cautious if venturing down onto the beach.

TRAILHEAD & LOOKOUT: N 48.139151, W 58.967167

In the community of Highlands, travel south along the main road through the community (Route 405) until the road becomes unpaved. Continue south for 2.5 kilometres to a small lookout on the right. A small, unmaintained staircase several hundred yards up the road provides beach access.

14. Red Rocks Building

Red Rocks, Cape Ray

Located at the base of the distinctive pointed mountains that make up Twin Hills north of Channel-Port aux Basques is the concrete shell of two buildings whose origins are a mystery. Some say the buildings belonged to a fire station that serviced the area. Given the large garage attached to the larger of the buildings, this seems plausible—but its location in the small abandoned community of Red Rocks makes this hypothesis unlikely. Red Rocks was a small settlement located at the northern reach of Cape Ray. Its residents were mainly fishers and farmers, with the exception of those employed to work on the area's communications systems.

In 1857, the first submarine cable came ashore in the community, connecting the island of Newfoundland to the mainland. From there, the line entered a repeater station before travelling across the island to St. John's. This was the beginning of telecommunications in the area. The next major installation was a 12-channel radio transmitter built on top of the nearby Sugar Loaf Mountain in 1950. From there, a direct connection to

Cape Breton could be achieved, increasing the reliability of the communication network to Nova Scotia. In 1958, the owners of the system, Canadian National Telecommunications, built another repeater building to support the mountaintop transmitter; this building is likely the one visible in the area today.

Located alongside the old railway bed and along the province-wide telegraph line, it seems likely that this was the building's main purpose. Whatever the original purpose of the building, today it is abandoned. The remnants are lasting reminders of the heritage of the settlement, now long gone, and its position along the bright blue waters of the Cabot Strait make it an excellent place to explore and hike.

RED ROCKS BUILDING: N 47.664419, W 59.308618
Approximately 18 kilometres north of Channel-Port aux Basques on the Trans-Canada Highway, turn onto a gravel road located next to Bear Cove Brook. Drive another 2 kilometres to arrive at the site.

15. MV *Sadie and Eva*
Channel-Port aux Basques

If you are lucky enough to visit Port aux Basques on a windless day, during low tide check out the sunken wreck of the cargo ship *Sadie and Eva*. Located at the bottom of a small cove on the north side of Grand Bay West, at the time of its launch in 1963 the MV *Sadie and Eva* was the largest ship ever constructed in the town.

The 227-tonne schooner, built by George Anderson and his sons, was 25.9 metres long and 6.7 metres wide. It spent its service life transporting fish, potatoes, salt, coal, and other goods to coastal communities of Newfoundland and Nova Scotia. In October 1970, the *Sadie and Eva* was on her last trip of the year to North Sydney when a fire broke out in the engine room. Although no one was injured, the ship was extensively damaged.

The ship spent a year in North Sydney before being purchased by T.J. Hardy, who owned the fish plant in Port aux Basques, and eventually towed it back to that community. Hardy let the ship fall into disrepair and it was towed to its final resting place.

Until the early 2010s, the ship's deteriorated wooden hull rose out of the water. But by the end of the decade, it had sunk beneath the waves. On a windless day, it is possible to glimpse the wooden skeleton of the ship.

MV *SADIE AND EVA*: N 47.599647, W 59.173742

Leaving from Dennis Road (N 47.603227, W 59.174252), walk about 330 metres along the Newfoundland T'Railway, where a wooden platform looks out over the cove.

Eddies Cove West
Port Saunders
Hawke's Bay
Englee
Fleur de Lys
La Scie
3
2
6
4
5
Jackson's Arm
1
Baie Verte
7
10
Hampden
Springdale
8
9
Triton
South Brook
Botwood
Badger
Grand Falls-Windsor

White Bay to Green Bay

White Bay, Baie Verte, & Green Bay

This region encompasses White Bay in the west, the Baie Verte Peninsula in the middle, and Green Bay and the western side of Notre Dame Bay in the east. The region has diverse landscapes, but a consistent history based on the changing industries and people's attempts to exploit the many resources the land has to offer. Mining, forestry, and hydroelectric production have helped some of the scattered communities to thrive. But the closure of mines and the difficulty in accessing much of the region has forced the resettlement of many places and transformed others into fragments of their former selves. This is perhaps best seen in the community of Tilt Cove, a once-thriving hub for mining in Notre Dame Bay given the title of Canada's smallest town in 2016 because of its population of four people.

This region was once part of the French Shore, regularly used by French fishers during the early years of European colonization. This legacy is apparent in the names of the major communities: La Scie, Fleur de Lys, and Baie Verte. But don't be fooled; the French were not first people to settle here. In the community of Fleur de Lys, visit the soapstone quarry where the Indigenous peoples known as the Maritime Archaic and

Dorset Paleo-Eskimo carved out bowls and tools some 4,000 and 1,500 years ago respectively. The Indigenous, French, and later English settlers of the land have always relied on the fishery, but in the 19th century the region's mineral potential began to be exploited in earnest. Mining continues to be a large part of the communities in the area, but it was not the only industry to affect the area. The construction of the Cat Arm Hydroelectric project in White Bay and continual logging operations in Hampden and Springdale provide vital infrastructure.

The region is an often overlooked and underappreciated part

of Newfoundland. Branching from the Trans-Canada Highway in the south, several highways provide access to its coastal communities. In the west, Route 420 winds up the west side of White Bay to the communities of Hampden, Sop's Arm, and Jackson's Arm. Farther east, Route 410 travels through the spine of the Baie Verte Peninsula, with many branching roads travelling to the communities located along the west, east, and north sides of the peninsula. To the east, Routes 390 and 380 explore the many bays, harbours, and towns that make up Southwest Arm, Green Bay, and Halls Bay.

1.   Sop's Arm Barge

Sop's Arm, White Bay

Situated in one of the small coves that make up the town of Sop's Arm is an abandoned barge of unknown origin. The rusting steel hull is pushed onto the shore, grounding the vessel, while the wooden superstructure comprised of multiple rooms and offices slowly deteriorates. Some say the barge was once part of the Corner Brook Pulp and Paper logging operations in the area, possibly to aid in the construction of the nearby Cat Arm Hydroelectric Facility. But it is more likely that the barge was used to aid in a pilot project to investigate the feasibility of helicopter logging in the area. Similar to the heli-logging operations in British Columbia, it was believed that heli-logging could be a viable way to access remote timber and forest in Newfoundland's

hard-to-reach areas. In 1999, the not-for-profit organization Newfoundland and Labrador Lumber Producers Association received $500,000 to begin operations. Part of this operation would have been to use the large barge as a base of operations for workers, helicopter refuelling, and storing/towing the timber.

After the project had concluded, it was determined that the small size of Newfoundland's forest meant that transporting logs by helicopter was not viable. The barge was run aground in the small cove to prevent it from being damaged by storms and ice floes.

What is known for certain is that in April 2010 the Canadian Coast Guard received a report that the barge was leaking oil; as a result, an environmental response team was deployed to drain the 550 litres of diesel fuel from the barge. After the cleanup was complete, the Coast Guard attempted to locate the owner in order to recover some of their costs, but they were unsuccessful. The case was later closed and the barge abandoned once again.

The barge remains grounded on the shores of the small cove. With each storm, the wooden structure atop the barge deteriorates a little more. Its rusting hull remains in relatively good condition but with little potential for possible future use, the barge is likely to remain abandoned.

 **SOP'S ARM BARGE:** N 49.783450, W 56.853431

Driving north of the Trans-Canada Highway on Route 420 to Jackson's Arm, travel about 50 kilometres to the Sop's Arm intersection. Turn right into the town and follow this road approximately 5.7 kilometres to its end. The barge is located across the harbour from the end of this road.

2. Coney Arm & Eastern Brook Falls

White Bay

Coney Arm is a community that has refused to become abandoned. Located north of Jackson's Arm, Coney Arm is nestled in the mountains and protected by a narrow outlet to White Bay. The beach-lined shores gradually change into flat forested fields before rising to form the sides of the valley, making it an ideal and protected place to build a house and dock a fishing vessel.

The community's population was never very high, with a maximum of 56 residents living there in the early 20th century. With time, Coney Arm's isolated location among the Long Range Mountains meant that access to the nearby trading outpost and amenities was severely limited. By 1954, all residents had resettled to nearby communities. The construction of a road to the Cat Arm Hydroelectric Plant north of Coney Arm provided new access to the harbour. This opened the community, and soon the harbour became a populated cabin community that remains to this day.

The tree-lined valley is another hidden gem of the Long Range Mountains that is worth a visit. Backdropping the community is Eastern Brook Falls, which cascades 60 metres over the valley side before draining into White Bay.

⊕ **CONEY ARM:** N 49.962830, W 56.790514

Just before entering the town of Jackson's Arm, turn onto the gravel road (N 49.853232, W 56.843807) leading toward Cat Arm. From here, travel 14.5 kilometres on the well-maintained road to arrive at Coney Arm.

3. Cat Arm Hydro Facility & Construction Tunnels

Cat Arm Hydroelectric Development, White Bay

Along the west side of White Bay on the inaccessible east coast of the Northern Peninsula is one of the island's largest hydroelectric developments. Beginning high in the Long Range Mountains, water contained by a series of dams enters an underground penstock before dropping 380 metres into the power generation station on the shores of White Bay.

Hidden within the scenery are remnants of the facility's 1981 construction. The most notable of these is an underground access tunnel, now hidden in the forest of the Long Range Mountains. The tunnel, large enough for a dump truck to drive through, was once used to access the underground excavation for the penstocks. The ghostly tunnel is fenced off for safety reasons.

Do not miss an opportunity to visit Cat Arm. The cove containing the hydroelectric generation station is an ideal place to experience White Bay; watch for the dozens of eagles and seabirds that nest on the coastal cliffs. The facility is still in operation and parts of the area are not only dangerous to visit but also forbidden. Obey all warning signs found throughout the active area.

CAT ARM HYDRO FACILITY: N 50.008448, W 56.763956

Immediately before entering Jackson's Arm on Route 420, turn west onto the gravel road toward the Cat Arm Hydroelectric Development. Travel approximately 21 kilometres on the well-maintained road to the road to the dam and generation facility.

4. Rattle Brook Spillway

Jackson's Arm, White Bay

This waterfall is special, not for its size or the amount of water flowing over it but for its exclusivity. During almost the entire year, Rattle Brook Falls is a small, barely visible trickle of water. The water flows over the rocky hillside before falling into Big Arm Brook gorge, north of the town of Jackson's Arm. The small cascading stream looks out of place against the 30-metre-wide riverbed through which it flows. This is because Rattle Brook Falls can only be truly experienced during high water levels or when maintenance is being done on the nearby Rattle Brook Hydroelectric Development.

Before the 1990s, water freely flowed over the 90-metre-high falls into the narrow gorge below. But in 1997 construction began on a small hydroelectric dam high on the mountain. The river was forced into a penstock and travels 1,100 metres to the small,

4-megawatt hydroelectric plant at the bottom of the valley. Now the only time the waterfall returns to life is when the spillway is needed due to high water levels or dam maintenance. Although the best time to watch for the spillway to be released is during spring runoff, it can be a difficult event to predict.

But the falls are worth seeing. The narrow gorge causes the main road passing through the area to the Cat Arm Hydroelectric Dam to pass worryingly close to the cliffside and spillway. During high runoff, the water flowing off the mountain crashes against the rocky hillside and pours onto the bridge before falling 40 metres into the gorge below.

RATTLE BROOK SPILLWAY: N 49.888676, W 56.836702
Immediately before entering the community of Jackson's Arm on Route 420, turn west onto the gravel road toward the Cat Arm Hydroelectric Development. Travel approximately 4.4 kilometres on the well-maintained road to reach the bridge across the spillway.

5. Tilt Cove Copper Mine
Baie Verte Peninsula

Perhaps it is now Canada's smallest town, but Tilt Cove was once one of the most prosperous mining communities in the province, igniting the mining boom that engulfed the Notre Dame Bay area. The seaside town is a shadow of its former self, but the legacy of the historic mining operation lives on.

HISTORY

Before 1857, Tilt Cove was a small fishing community. Then Smith McKay began prospecting along the coast of Notre Dame Bay. McKay met a fisher named Isaac Windsor, who showed him an outcrop of copper ore near the small cove. McKay, together with Charles Bennett, who owned and operated mines around the province, formed the Union Mining Company in 1864.

Mining operations began almost immediately. On July 27, 1864, the first blast occurred at the Union Mine (also called the West Mine). After being extracted by explosives and manual labour, the ore was transported by a series of cable cars along an iron tramway to a wharf. From here, it was shipped to smelters in Swansea, England. Tilt Cove was the epicentre of mining activity. Centred around the small pond named Windsor Lake, the mine and communituy were nestled in a small valley along the shores of Notre Dame Bay.

The initial success of the Tilt Cove Mine did not go unnoticed and soon many new mining operations and exploration began in the Notre Dame Bay area. The mine was not void of trouble, however, the first of which was experienced in 1880 when a

dispute between McKay and Bennett led to Bennett's purchasing McKay's ownership of the mine. As a result, the mine came under the ownership of the Cape Copper Company. Soon afterward, the mine experienced difficulties extracting the high-quality ore required by the English smelters. Mining operations slowed and the population of the town diminished, as workers moved to neighbouring mines.

In 1883, Charles Bennett passed away. With no set plan in place, his trustees leased the mine and its equipment to the London-based company Tilt Cove Copper Company Ltd. in 1888. This company built a smelter on the site but the high cost of coal made the endeavour unfeasible, and the smelter was scrapped shortly after its construction.

Around the same, engineers determined that removing further ore from the Union Mine would compromise the mine's structural integrity. To solve this problem, a new mine was commissioned in 1886, named the East Mine. The East Mine contained significant amounts of sulphur, gold, and silver.

In 1890, the East Mine was leased to the Cape Copper Company Ltd., which returned to shipping the ore to the original smelters in England. The West Mine was also reopened for a short period, and the town experienced its second boom. In 1901, there were four churches, three schools, and nearly 250 houses in Tilt Cove.

The West Mine shut down in 1902 due to the depletion of accessible minerals. In 1914, the Tilt Cove Copper Company went bankrupt and returned the land lease to Bennett's trustees.

The mine operated briefly again during World War I, when copper prices increased, but closed soon after. By the 1920s, Tilt Cove was once again no more than a quiet fishing village. In 1957, the Tilt Cove mine was reopened by the First Maritime Mining Corporation, and although this opening did not bring the same expansion to the town as it had previously experienced, it operated successfully for 10 years before depleted ore reserves forced it to shut down once again.

In post-mining Tilt Cove, residents made a living through boat building and fishing but, over time, even this small population diminished. Tilt Cove remains a recognized town, but with a population of only four residents. Since 2000, the mine and remaining reserves have caught the attention of multiple companies, but no mining operation has ensued.

ABOUT THE AREA

Tilt Cove is situated among the steep forested hills, and while it is sheltered among these crater-like mountains, a narrow valley allows access to the coast, providing views of the rugged coastal cliffs.

The houses of current residents are largely confined to the east side of the narrow valley, but for most of its history most of the town was located on the west side, where several houses and buildings can still be viewed. Little remains of the community and what does is shadowed by the vast scars and remnants of the mining operation.

The barren, gravel hillsides are stained with copper and rust. Steep rock cuts and large excavation sites on both sides of the valley mark the location of the main mining area. Near the water, remnants of the large wharf and storage facilities are visible, along with the signs of tunnels and holes in the coastal cliffs.

Several clearly marked concrete, capped mine shafts are visible. While it may be tempting to explore a little closer, the depth of each shaft should be enough to deter closer investigation— some are more than 880 metres deep (a distance greater than the height of Newfoundland's tallest mountains).

Tilt Cove resembles a ghost town haunted by the surrounding mine. Be sure to visit to experience the story of how one of Newfoundland's most successful mines turned into Canada's smallest town.

TILT COVE COPPER MINE: N 49.886891, W 55.631454 Approximately 6.1 kilometres west of the community of La Scie on Route 414, turn onto a small dirt road heading south. Travel another 5.7 kilometres to arrive at Tilt Cove.

6.   Baie Verte Asbestos Mine
Baie Verte Peninsula

The damaging effects of asbestos are well known today, and no one knows this better than those who worked in the Baie Verte Asbestos Mine. Today the mine site offers a combination of steep cliffs, beautifully coloured rocks, and crystal blue lakes, but the dark legacy of its past and the significance it holds in the fight for workers' rights cannot be forgotten.

Although asbestos mining in the area dates to the late 19th century, the modern mine known today was established after the discovery of a large asbestos outcrop approximately 4 kilometres north of the community of Baie Verte in 1955. Advocate Mines established an open-pit mine in 1963. Throughout the 1970s, the health impacts of asbestos became better understood and the union representing mine workers pushed for better safety protection against the dangerous conditions. A comprehensive study completed by world-renowned specialist Dr. Irving Solikoff determined that a significant portion of the workforce exhibited asbestos-related diseases and recommended steps to ensure the safety of the mine workers. The mine claimed that the cost of the safety measures would negatively affect the viability of the mine and, with the backing of the provincial Minister of Mines and future premier Brian Peckford, insisted that it was not necessary.

The workers, worried for their safety, went on strike; it lasted 14 days and was accompanied by an enormous public outcry. It was the first strike in Canada taken exclusively for the occupational health and safety of workers. The mining company eventually succumbed to the workers' demands. But by 1980,

the mine experienced difficulty accessing the high-grade ore located deep beneath its surface. As well, the dangers of asbestos became better understood, and, in 1981, the mine was forced to shut down. Although it was opened again the following year by Transpacific Asbestos Ltd., the decreasing demand for asbestos material, the associated health and safety risks, and the ore's inaccessibility forced the closure of the mine in 1990.

ABOUT THE AREA

The Baie Verte Asbestos Mine is a story of tremendous pain and suffering for many workers and people in nearby Baie Verte, one that has a sombre end for far too many. And even though this will not soon be forgotten, the landscape holds a certain irony: the open-pit mine is an ominous place and an environmental disaster, but it is also a spectacular sight. The light-coloured asbestos mineral produces incredible shades of blue and turquoise in the flooded pit, contradicting the dark rocks that line the cliffs and

tailings piles. Rising high above the rest of the landscape, they can best be described as barren mountains.

Much of the equipment and facilities that once made up this mine has long been removed, but the barren landscape, steep excavated cliffs, and deep, turquoise water bodies are a worthwhile sight. Be aware, however, that the dangers of blowing dust and the conditions left over from the mine are not to be taken lightly.

Luckily, the best of the Baie Verte Mine can be viewed from the rim of the pit, where Route 410 and a small, designated lookout provide panoramic views of the area.

BAIE VERTE ASBESTOS MINE: N 49.968971, W 56.183065
The mine is located about 5 kilometres north of the town of Baie Verte, immediately adjacent to Route 410. The best views of the mine are from a lookout (N 49.979952, W 56.198242) located along the roadway.

7. King's Point Rattling Brook Falls

Rattling Brook, Green Bay

Rattling Brook Falls has long been called one of Newfoundland's geologic wonders. The waterfall drops off the mountainous plateau that surrounds the southwest arm and falls almost 140 metres before flowing into the harbour. The falls can be difficult to see at times, as it is located in a narrow gorge carved into the dark, 440-million-year-old rocks. The best time to see the falls is during high water runoff in the early spring. Local communities have built a short hiking trail and viewing platforms alongside the falls, allowing visitors to get the most out of their visit.

RATTLING BROOK FALLS: N 49.620884, W 56.176084
The trailhead to the falls is located just before entering the town of Rattling Brook, approximately 3.6 kilometres north of King's Point. The falls are visible via a 500-metre-long hike to a lookout point.

8. Glassy Beach

Springdale

Hidden in the nooks and crannies of Halls Bay is a little cove with a beach filled with smooth, gently eroded sea glass. The beach was formed from years of waste being disposed into the Springdale waterfront. Over time, the glass and ceramics in this waste was slowly eroded by the continuous wave movement in the bay and eventually pushed ashore to form the secluded little beach. The beach, an extraordinary wonder produced by years

of environmental carelessness, is at risk of disappearing. It takes years for shards of glass to break up, smoothen, and be deposited on the beach. As each person takes a piece of glass from the beach, the glass depletes. Please leave the glass for all to enjoy.

 **GLASSY BEACH:** N 49.514906, W 56.013473

The beach is located in the town of Springdale at the end of Main Street (Route 390). Signs to the beach, found at the end of the road, guide you to the short trail to the beach.

9. Pilley's Island Mine
Pilley's Island

What remains of the Pilley's Island Mine is only a small portion of the successful endeavour that was once Newfoundland's largest pyrite mine. The mine, whose ore was smelted for decades for iron, copper, and sulphur, was one of the major employers in the area, which helped establish many of the towns in the area. The mineral potential of the area was first noted in the 1860s. A rusty yellow pattern in the rocks along the shore resulted in one nearby cove being named Bumble Bee Bight, and led Philip Cleary to purchase the mineral rights for the area around the same time.

The mine had a difficult beginning, with several transfers of ownerships and unsuccessful attempts to extract the ore. The Pyrites Company Limited purchased the mine in 1891 and began constructing new mine shafts, buildings, and tramways. The endeavour paid off and, over the next nine years, 270,000 tons of ore that was sent to smelters in Canada and the US were extracted. Due to increasing difficulty in accessing the ore deep underground, the mine was sold to the Newfoundland Exploration Syndicate, which successfully mined 218,000 tons of ore between 1902 and 1908. In 1908, the mine was no longer viable and was shut down. In 1914, most of its equipment was auctioned off to be used as scrap metal to aid the war in Europe.

The mine was located beside a large pond, now named Mine Pond. Today large pieces of equipment are visible along the shore, and in the hills surrounding the pond pieces of the long-gone buildings and the mine's wooden supports protrude from the yellow-stained hillside.

 **PILLEY'S ISLAND MINE:** N 49.508253, W 55.719523

Driving north, go approximately 500 metres past the Bumblebee Bight Inn and Brewery on Main St. (Route 380). Turn onto Mine's Pond Road; almost immediately, there is a small parking lot and an informative sign that marks the start of the mine.

10. Little Bay Islands
Notre Dame Bay

It is probably too early to declare Little Bay Islands an abandoned community in the traditional sense, but as of 2021, it is Newfoundland's most recently resettled community. The community is nestled in a small, protected harbour on the west side of Little Bay Islands. For nearly 200 years, European settlers made a living in the community from fishing and boatbuilding.

The first permanent residents arrived in 1825, when a single family moved to the area to access the Notre Dame Bay fishing grounds. By 1845, the first census revealed that 45 people lived there, all involved with the inshore fishery. The community soon became a hub for trading, fishing, and boatbuilding in Notre Dame Bay. The local cod fishery, in addition to the seal, herring, and lobster fisheries, provided the necessary jobs and income for the community to grow. The population of 560 people in 1935 held steady until the second half of the 20th century. While there was a short burst of immigration to the community due to the establishment of a crab and seal factory, fish plant, and shipyard in the 1970s, the general population trend was downward after 1950. As is the case for so many communities, more opportunities for work, education, and amenities in nearby communities forced people to relocate.

In February 2019, the remaining 55 residents voted to accept the provincial government's $250,000 minimum payout offer to relocate. By December of the following year, all but two residents had moved; the final two decided to remain in the abandoned community. Seemingly overnight, the community was all but abandoned. Dozens of historically significant buildings including the fish plant, schoolhouse, houses, and stores remain.

The community is not totally abandoned and likely will not be for some time. Although many houses and buildings will never be used again, just as many are likely to become cabins and summer homes to those who once lived in them. Visit this isolated island in one of Newfoundland's most treacherous bays, as no resettled community can offer the cultural and built heritage that remains dormant in this small town.

 **LITTLE BAY ISLANDS:** N 49.641831, W 55.790776

Getting to the community is not possible without a boat. The nearest communities are Lushes Bight, located on a nearby island, and Beachside, north of Springdale. As of 2021, no official tours of the island are provided.

Deer Lake
Botwood
Bishop's Falls
Badger
Grand Falls-Windsor
Buchans
Millertown
St. Alban's
Hermitage
Burgeo
Grey River
Francois
Ramea
Harbour Breton
1
2
3
4
5
6
7

Central Newfoundland

Central Newfoundland & the South Coast

CENTRAL/INTERIOR OF NEWFOUNDLAND

Central Newfoundland challenges the idea that Newfoundland is solely a barren, rocky landscape along the ocean. The vast, unexplored backcountry that makes up most of Central Newfoundland contains dense forest and extensive wetlands. Newfoundland's largest river, the Exploits River, runs through the heart of Newfoundland. Beginning at Red Indian Lake and flowing to Botwood Bay, it powers the forestry industry that has helped establish the communities of Badger, Grand Falls-Windsor, and Botwood. The size and turbulence of the river did not stop the Beothuk from conquering it, using the river for transportation and fishing.

Today the area has become a pass-through for many, but you do not want to miss its communities, culture, and landscape. The region's uninhabited wilderness means that there is plenty to explore for those willing to look.

Central Newfoundland was the primary home of the Beothuk. Most of what we know about these people came from the captured Desmasduit and her niece Shanawdithit. By the time the government began prospecting their land for resources and planning construction of a railway in the mid- to late 19th century, these Indigenous peoples had been killed off.

The Newfoundland railway opened up access to the forest and land of Central Newfoundland and quickly led to the establishment of the Grand Falls Pulp and Paper Mill. The area continued to boom when zinc, lead, and copper were discovered in the soon-to-be-established company town of Buchans. The region diversified even more when a seaplane base was built in the coastal town of Botwood and later expanded during World War II. The history and heritage of Central Newfoundland is as diverse as its landscape.

This expansive region is an outdoors person's oasis. Best explored by snowmobile or ATV, the region also offers plenty of hiking trails and driving routes. The Trans-Canada Highway connects the towns of Badger, Grand Falls-Windsor, and Bishop's Falls. In the west from Badger, Route 370 travels to Millertown and Buchans. Farther east, Botwood is accessible by Route 350, and just south of this intersection on the Trans-Canada Highway is the beginning of the remote Route 360 highway to Bay d'Espoir and the south coast.

SOUTH COAST OF NEWFOUNDLAND

While Central Newfoundland may challenge perceptions of the typical Newfoundland landscape, the south coast illuminates them. With rolling barren hills plunging through inaccessible valleys into the exposed ocean, the land appears completely inhospitable. But this has not stopped the resilient people who settled in the few relatively flat areas and sheltered harbours. Fishing continues to be the primary industry. The region has been shaped by the establishment of merchant towns such as Harbour Breton, which served the isolated communities that dot the coast. Today the region is a hidden wonder that few tourists or Newfoundlanders and Labradorians have explored.

The south coast depended on the Grand Banks fishery. Many residents settled within the protected harbours of Bay d'Espoir or along the fingerlike peninsulas reaching into Fortune Bay. Settlements are also found along the coast between the Burin Peninsula and Port aux Basques. This area relied heavily on the coastal boat service for supplies and market access, but over time some isolated south coast communities were resettled. Francois, Grey River, and the island community of Ramea remain accessible only by the provincial ferry service.

There are three ways to access the south coast. Near the town of Bishop's Falls, Route 360 travels to Bay d'Espoir and the communities of Hermitage and Harbour Breton. Each is rich in history, culture, and scenery. From here, provincial ferry services provide access to Recontre East via Pool's Cove, and to Gaultois, McCallum, and Francois via Hermitage. The second option is to take Route 480, which begins near Stephenville on Newfoundland's west coast and leads to Burgeo. Known for having some of the best beaches in Newfoundland, Burgeo offers ferry services to Ramea, Grey River, and Francois. Finally, from Rose Blanche-Habour le Cou on Route 470, west of Channel-Port aux Basques, a small ferry services La Poile.

1. The Topsails

Central Newfoundland

There are few places in Newfoundland where the phrase alien landscape is more applicable than on the Topsails. The high barren land appears as a smooth, flat rock shield when looking down upon it, with the exception of four obscure lumps of rock rising from the plateau named Main Topsail, Mizzen Topsail, Gaff Topsail, and Fore Topsail. The Topsails rise approximately 61 to 122 metres and are visible from miles away. In the winter, the area is notorious for high winds and incredible snowdrifts.

FORMATION

The Topsails are a geologic feature known as a tor, monadock, or inselberg, which is an isolated hill of bedrock that rises above the surrounding area, formed when a section of bedrock contains

stronger and more erosion-resistant rock than the surrounding landscape and thus do not degrade as quickly. Much of the plateau surrounding the Topsails is covered in bogs, wetland, and small shrubs, but at higher elevations the smooth barren rock has some soil and vegetation found in rock depressions.

The smooth and featureless rock is the result of glacier movement during the last ice age, approximately 10,000 to 12,000 years ago. Because this is the highest point in the area, much of the ice covering the land is believed to have dispersed radially from this location.

PEOPLE'S HISTORY

The first people to have been active in the area were the Beothuk, who resided in locations near Red Indian Lake to the east and Grand Lake in the west.

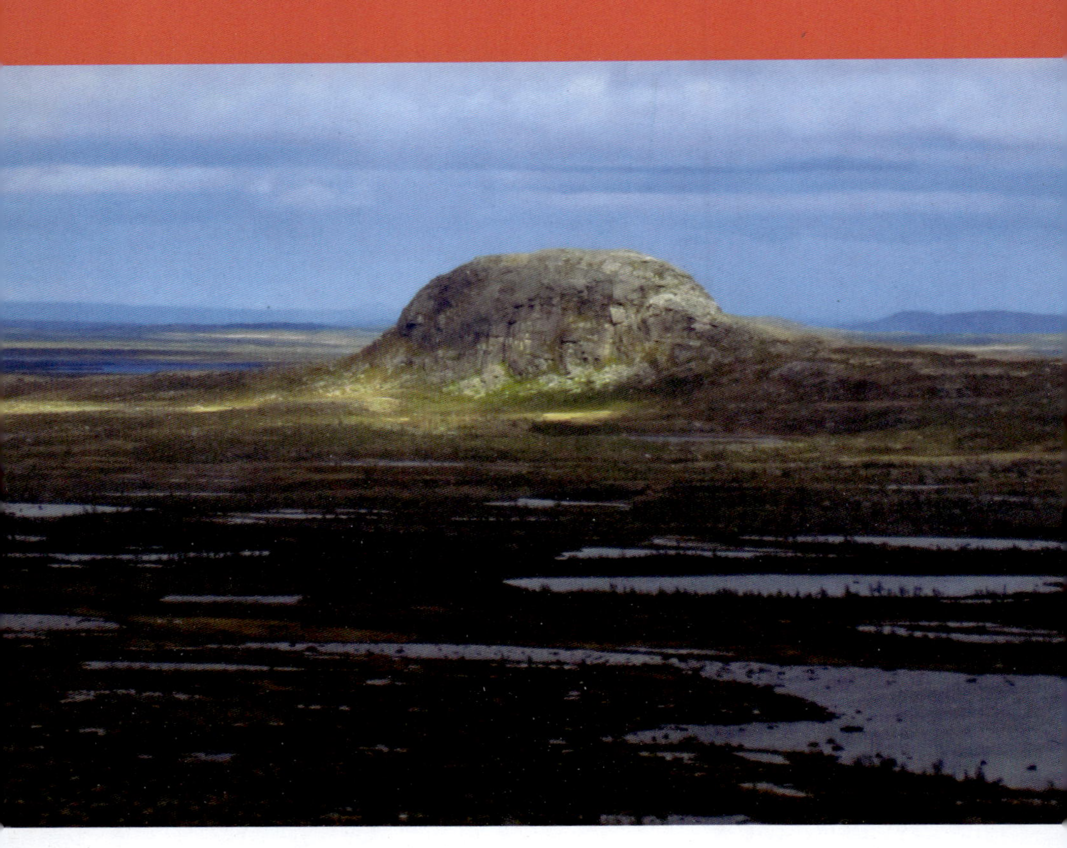

Many of the first European expeditions across the province financed by the British government, such as those by James P. Howley, mention the Topsails, but it was not until the area was surveyed for railway construction that any substantial information about the area was recorded. As construction began, homes were built along the railway tracks and, by 1911, the town was recorded on a census as "Topsails."

The railway was constructed through the Topsails between 1893 and 1897. This stretch of railway was the highest on the island and this, combined with the treacherous winds experienced on the barren plateau and the heavy snow accumulation, meant that this section was one of the toughest sections to construct and maintain.

Nearby, several granite quarries were opened and supplied

most of the stone needed for railway bridge abutments and even the construction of the St. John's Railway Station.

However, the community's low population, difficult accessibility, and reclassification of the railway section from "manned" to "unmanned" in the early 1950s resulted in it being abandoned between 1951 and 1956. The railway was closed in the 1980s.

The struggle to clear the tracks of snow and maintain the route over the Topsails contributed to the decision to decommission the railway. In its day, however, the route provided critical access to the forestry and mineral resources of the west coast.

ABOUT THE AREA

Today, the Main Topsail, Mizzen Topsail, Gaff Topsail, and Fore Topsail rise above the surrounding landscape. The region is accessible by snowmobile or ATV by using the Newfoundland T'Railway. Although the winds can be unrelenting, during good weather a hike to the most accessible topsail, the Gaff, provides panoramic views of the region. For those wishing to hike a little farther, the remaining Topsails are hikeable.

 **TRAILHEAD TO GAFF TOPSAIL: N 49.138280, W 56.634275**

From the trailhead in Howley (N 49.168374, W 57.109308), travel east along the Newfoundland T'Railway for approximately 39 kilometres to arrive next to the Gaff Topsail.

From the trailhead in Badger (N 48.979751, W 56.046788), travel west along the Newfoundland T'Railway for approximately 62 kilometres to the area.

LUCKY STRIKE MINE
1927 - 1979
DISCOVERY SITE NO. 2

2. Buchans Mine

Buchans, Central Newfoundland

Located in the wilderness of Central Newfoundland, the town of Buchans was built entirely to support the area's mining operation. Lead, zinc, and copper mines helped the community thrive through the 20th century and became a critical economic booster not only to the area but to the entire province. Over time, the viability of the mines decreased and were shut down. Today, Buchans is on the list of Newfoundland and Labrador towns that have transformed from a bustling boomtown to a quiet community, scarred with a historic landscape of abandoned buildings and relics.

HISTORY

The history of Buchans begins with the formation of the Anglo-Newfoundland Development Company (AND Company) in 1905. After the first phases of constructing a pulp and paper mill in nearby Grand Falls, the company hired prospectors to determine the mineral potential of the surrounding lands: Mi'kmaq guide, explorer, and prospector Mattie Mitchell began prospecting the Red Indian Lake area.

While exploring along the banks of the Buchans River in 1905, Mitchell discovered ore bodies containing zinc, lead, copper, gold, and silver. He was given $2.50 by the company.

The ore Mitchell discovered was an interlaced mixture of rock and the desired minerals. The available technology could not extract the desired minerals at the time. The AND Company is reported to have extracted small amounts of ore between 1905 and 1911, but much of it was discarded due to the high concentrations of impurities.

In 1916, H.A. Guess, vice-president of the American Smelting and Refining Company (ASARCO), learned of the ore discovery and collected further samples for testing and experimentation. The company worked on new methods to extract the ore and, in 1926, made a deal with AND: ASARCO would manage and process the ore in exchange for 50 per cent of the profits being returned to AND.

Workers quickly laid the groundwork for the operation and through the summer prospectors discovered the ore bodies known as "Lucky Strike" and "Oriental." Underground shafts were dug, and mining was under way before the following year. In January 1927, the Buchans Mining Company was established and work began on constructing a town adjacent to the mining site.

Three years later, in 1928, the first lead ore was ready for shipment. To deliver it to market, a 35-kilometre-long railway line connecting the mines to the port facilities in Botwood was constructed. Shortly after production began, the Great Depression

occurred, and ASARCO had to decide whether to shut down the mine or double its production in order to keep the mine viable. The latter option was chosen and the mine experienced a huge boom in production.

The mine's first employees resided in bunkhouses, log cabins, and canvas tents. By 1928, 60 houses, a post office, hospital, and several churches had been constructed. Public schools were opened shortly after, and by the 1960s, Buchans contained a swimming pool, bowling alley, tennis court, and curling rink. But, all facilities, houses, and amenities were owned and controlled by ASARCO.

The mine was only ever expected to be short-lived but further discoveries resulted in continued operations until 1984. Before shutting down, the mine experienced several major strikes as workers demanded better safety standards, wages, and living conditions. In 1975, when the workers began forming the first unions, the company officially announced its phase-down operations.

In July 1977, company houses were put up for sale and most of the workers laid off. Some mining operations and exploration ventures continued over the next few years and the discovery of another ore body resulted in mining operations between 1983 and 1984, but in September 1984 all production was halted and the mine closed for good. By the end of the mine's 57-year operation, it had produced approximately 17.5 million tons of ore, grossing over $14 billion, making it one of the most productive and richest sulphide mines in the world—all because of Mattie Mitchell, who was paid $2.50 for discovering the ore and who was not recognized for that discovery until after his death in 1922.

ABOUT THE AREA

Buchans is full of artifacts and reminders of its past self. After the mine closure, the town's population dwindled, but today a sustained population of about 650 people work and live there.

The Buchans Miner's Museum tells the fascinating history of the town and walks visitors through preserved construction equipment, train cars, and mining equipment on the museum grounds. Explore the town, where numerous restored ore cars, excavators, and some of the mines themselves have been left as monuments to its history and culture.

The most notable image of Buchans is that of the Lucky Strike mine's headframe (a derrick-like tower that serviced the underground shaft) and adjacent processing buildings overlooking a large "pond." The water body, named Glory Hole, is a flooded open-pit mine that reaches depths of up to 30 metres. The mine and nearby buildings are now used for storage. A building nearby,

owned by Barite Mud Services, houses operations to remediate the mine's tailings piles and extract the barite from the rock.

While many houses in Buchans have been vacated, the perfectly laid out, company-built town still reflects its past. Many of its churches, commercial buildings, and schools still exist, and along the perimeter of the town, ore and equipment storage buildings have been repurposed.

Gravel roads, ATV trails, and snowmobile trails allow exploration of the town's former airfield, hydroelectric facility, and the mining sites located farther from the town.

BUCHANS MINE: N 48.825196, W 56.851432

The mine is located in the heart of Buchans. From Badger on the Trans-Canada Highway, travel approximately 73 kilometres south along Route 370 to Buchans

3. Thunder Brook Falls

Grand Falls-Windsor

During the summer, Thunder Brook, also called Leech Brook, attracts hundreds of swimmers from Grand Falls-Windsor and Badger. This swimming spot is located on the side of the Trans-Canada Highway, 10 kilometres west of Grand Falls-Windsor. From the parking lot located on the north side of the highway, a short hike takes you to the first swimming area. Just past this shallow wading pool, the river enters a narrow gorge with a large waterfall at its far end. The hiking trail takes you along the rim of the gorge to a second waterfall. Two deep swimming areas here allow swimmers to swim up and under the waterfalls. The falls are worth a visit. On rare, hot days, it is a lovely place for a swim or a picnic.

 **FIRST SWIMMING HOLE:** N 48.947733, W 55.829371

The trailhead (N 48.945516, W 55.828302) and parking lot to the swimming location and falls are located approximately 10 kilometres west of Grand Falls-Windsor, on the east side of Thunder Brook Bridge. A small ATV trail leads 150 metres to the first swimming location. From here, a short, moderate hike is required to the first and second waterfalls (the second and third swimming locations), located 150 metres and 300 metres away, respectively.

4. Botwood's Seaplane Base
Botwood, Central Newfoundland

For most of its history, Botwood's economy centred around the shipping of ore from the mines in Buchans and paper and supplies to and from the Grand Falls mill. But between 1937 and 1945, the town became home to a seaplane base that operated as a refuelling point for transatlantic aircraft.

Remnants of the base are visible throughout the town. The aircraft loading/parking area, seaplane ramp, and magazine bunkers on Killick Island are visible from the waterfront.

HISTORY

The small town of Botwood experienced its first major growth spurt when it began shipping pulp and paper from the Grand Falls mill. Its next came after a 1935 agreement between Canada, Ireland, and the United Kingdom to develop a transatlantic air service. Newfoundland was chosen as the western terminus for

these flights and an airfield was constructed at Gander and a seaplane base in Botwood.

Construction began soon after the agreement was signed and, in the spring of 1937, the Botwood Seaplane Base was completed. It contained all the facilities a traditional airfield required: administration buildings, maintenance shops, fuel storage, meteorological facilities, a passenger lounge, and accommodations. Because the base was used exclusively by seaplanes, no runway was constructed. Instead, a ramp that would allow aircraft to land on and take off from the Bay of Exploits and unload passengers and their cargo was built.

Botwood experienced many changes during World War II. With the outbreak of war, the aircraft using the base were exclusively under military and government charter, leading to an increased demand for security there. In June 1940, 852 men of the Canadian Reserve Infantry Regiment (nicknamed Black Watch) arrived at Botwood to provide security and defence. The men were armed with only rifles and therefore could only defend

against low-level aircraft attacks or infantry raids. As time went on, more soldiers were brought in to be trained.

By August 1940, a request to expand the Botwood base was sent to the Newfoundland government. Soon afterward, construction began on upgrading the airport's infrastructure. The Canadian Reserve Regiment known as the Queens Own Rifles of Canada arrived in Botwood from Camp Borden, Ontario, and the Black Watch were relocated to Gander. Several more changes to the battalions and regiments protecting Botwood occurred before the end of World War II.

The base expansion began in spring 1941. The 40-foot-long ramp and apron area were upgraded and two large seaplane hangars, a hospital, additional barracks, repair shops, and new water supply systems were constructed. Ammunition bunkers were built on Killick Island and two coastal defence batteries were built at Phillips Head and the lesser-known Wisemans Head.

It is estimated that 10,000 soldiers passed through Botwood between 1940 and 1945. As the war ended, so did the need for a

large military presence at Botwood. The Canadian troops stationed there were relocated, and most of the base was dismantled, relocated, and/or sold. World War II also brought rapid advances in land-based aircraft and the decline of flying boats. As a result, the Botwood Seaplane Base was also decommissioned.

Many of the remaining buildings and land were handed over to the Government of Newfoundland for a pittance. One such building was the 100-bed hospital, which was sold to the government for $1 in 1946, and which operated until 1989.

SEAPLANE BASE: N 49.152449, W 55.341560

The town of Botwood is located approximately 15 kilometres north of the Trans-Canada Highway near Bishop's Falls along Route 350. Turn right onto Fernwood Drive to enter the town. The seaplane base is located near the harbour (N 49.152449, W 55.341560) along with the causeway to Killick Island.

5. Phillips Head & Wisemans Head Battery

Botwood Bay

During World War II, fears that enemy U-boats or aircraft would attack the Botwood Seaplane Base and cripple the transatlantic seaplane service grew. The Canadian military constructed two coastal defence batteries between 1940 and 1941. The batteries were placed on opposite sides of Botwood Bay at Phillips Head and Wisemans Head and staffed by the 106th Coast Battery Royal Canadian Artillery.

Both batteries were constructed with reinforced concrete walls and covered in backfill to provide some camouflage from aircraft flying overhead. Built behind the battery, hidden in the forest, wooden-frame barracks, storage buildings, and generator buildings supported the main battery and were connected by underground tunnels.

The Phillips Head Battery consisted of a 4.7-inch gun and was operational in the summer of 1941. This defence battery contained 11 rooms connected by nearly 200 metres of underground passages and a three-storey lookout tower for a 360-degree view of the area.

On the opposite side of the bay is the larger Wisemans Head Battery, which contained a 10-inch gun and was operational by December 1941. This enormous battery was similar in size to the one at Cape Spear, near St. John's.

◎ **PHILLIPS HEAD BATTERY:** N 49.225568, W 55.304151

Leaving from Botwood (Route 350), exit the Trans-Canada Highway near Bishop's Falls, and drive approximately 20 kilometres on Route 350. Veer right onto Route 352 and continue for 8 kilometres. A sign marking the start of the short trail (N 49.225741, W 55.304363) to the battery is located on the right.

◎ **WISEMANS HEAD BATTERY:** N 49.231322, W 55.228763

From the town of Lewisporte, travel approximately 16 kilometres on Route 341 toward Laurenceton. Park on the side of the highway, around N 49.223400, W 55.215844. From here a 1.5-kilometre-long backcountry hike is required. There is no trail directly to the site.

6. Fjords of the South Coast
Grey River, Francois, McCallum, & Gaultois

Some of Newfoundland's most astonishing hidden gems are the steep valleys and fjords that make up its south coast. The entire coast is relatively isolated, with only a few communities reachable by car and a few only reachable by the provincial ferry services. But those with the opportunity to explore this coast are greeted with some of the most stunning coastlines of Newfoundland.

The best way to experience all the nooks and hidden coves of the south coast is either by long-distance hiking or by boat. The next best option is to use the provincial ferry system that guides visitors to the isolated communities of Grey River, Francois, McCallum, and Gaultois.

One of the top destinations is Grey River. As the ferry leaves the island community of Ramea, it heads toward the towering cliffs of the south coast. Several hundred metres from crashing into the cliff a small passageway reveals itself and the boat goes through the narrow fjord.

Grey River is located at the bottom of steep, forested hills about halfway through the fjord. A short hike or paddle farther up the valley reveals a huge network of inland bays and valleys.

If you continue on the ferry to Francois, you are greeted with similar awe-inspiring landscapes. Except this time, the steep fjords are distinguished by barren mountains; hiking beyond the community you arrive at panoramic views of the sea and the fjords that wind down into it.

These communities are accessible using the provincial ferry service from either Burgeo or Hermitage. All except one ferry carry vehicles; however, the only community with driveable roads is Ramea, and even it can be traversed easily by foot. Each community along the south coast is very small but contains nightly house rentals or places to camp.

BURGEO

Burgeo is located approximately 213 kilometres south of Corner Brook. From here one of two ferries brings you to Ramea, Grey River, and/or Francois. Be sure to check the schedule as they make

certain routes at certain times depending on the time of year and day of the week. As of the time of this writing, the ferry to Francois makes a trip to McCallum once a week.

HERMITAGE

Hermitage is located approximately 220 kilometres south of Grand Falls-Windsor. A ferry makes regular trips to Gaultois and McCallum. Once a week the ferry servicing Francois makes a trip to McCallum, allowing access to the communities farther west.

7.   Grey River Tungsten Mine

Grey River, South Coast

On the east side of the charming community of Grey River is a small entrance to a horizontal mine shaft. This small mine began when local trapper Henry Roose sent samples containing cassiterite and silver to the Buchans Mining Company Ltd. in 1954, sparking extensive prospecting. A rich vein, named Number 10, was discovered to contain vast amounts of tungsten.

To obtain further data on the mineral potential of the area, a 1,920-metre-long exploration adit (horizontal tunnel) was excavated into the hillside between 1966 and 1969. The 2.4 by 2.4-metre tunnel was excavated and mined using a cart and narrow-gauge track system run by a small diesel motor. A bunkhouse and mess hall built in Grey River provided housing for the miners, as well as a wharf, generator house, repair shop, and other support buildings.

Twenty-six samples or 275 tons were extracted from inside the hill and the mineral grade tested. The company had planned to continue mining the mineral vein but in 1970 the price of tungsten dropped, and the project was not deemed viable.

The claim expired in 2000. South Coast Ventures staked the claim and, in 2004, it was transferred again to Playfair Minerals. The following year, Playfair Minerals re-examined previous prospecting expeditions and took samples from the area. In 2011, the company reported that the mine had significant potential; however, no further mining has been done to date.

The mine entrance is easily located by walking along the eastern shore of the community. The entrance is perfectly intact and, in the surrounding area, mine carts, tracks, and rusted equipment are visible.

MINE ENTRANCE: N 47.589524, W 57.100265
From the Grey River ferry dock, hike approximately 200 metres on a dirt road along the east side of the bay to reach the mine.

Fogo Island
Twillingate
Moreton's Harbour
Musgrave Harbour
Lumsden
Main Point-Davidsville
Lewisporte
Greenspond
Glenwood
Gander
Hare Bay
Gambo
Port Blandford
Clarenville
5
7
6
3
4
1
2
9
8
10

Lewisporte to Bonavista Bay

Gander, Twillingate, & the Road to the Beaches

In the west of this diverse region, hundreds of harbours, coves, and islands line the Bay of Exploits. Twillingate and Fogo, two of the island's most popular tourist destinations, are also two of the best places for iceberg and whale watching. Continuing east, the rocky coastline transforms into the beautiful beaches found around Musgrave Harbour. Farther south, the town of Gander, once called the "crossroads of the world" for its importance to transatlantic aviation, continues to thrive—though its aviation culture has been replaced by its new role as a supply hub for the area.

The story of the region begins with the Beothuk who, for hundreds of years, used the area to hunt, fish, and live. In Boyd's Cove, the Beothuk Interpretation Centre walks you through the history and culture of these first inhabitants. The fishery led to the first established communities; however, soon industries such as mining emerged. Ocean travel was vital to the region, resulting in many shipwrecks along its coast, some of which are still visible today.

In the late 19th century, the Newfoundland Railway opened up the interior of the island to the south. Initially, this did not effect much change, but the constantly evolving aviation industry soon required Newfoundland to act as a transfer and refuelling point for transatlantic aircraft. The location that would become Gander—close to the railway and allowing for easy shipment of people and materials—was chosen to host what would become, for a time, the world's largest airport.

The Trans-Canada Highway is the main route east and west. From the highway, three routes access the Bay of Exploits and the north shore. Route 340 travels through Lewisporte and Birchy Bay and on to Boyd's Cove, Summerford, and Twillingate. Turn off Route 340 near Boyd's Cove onto Route 331 to access the ferry to Change Islands and Fogo Island (via Route 335) or travel to Gander Bay and connect to Route 330. Route 330 travels north of Gander and loops around Musgrave Harbour and Lumsden before turning into Route 320 and travelling through the communities of New-Wes-Valley and Hare Bay, and ending in Gambo back at the Trans-Canada Highway.

089366

1. HMS *Calypso/Briton*

Jobs Cove, Embree & Indian Arm

An enormous rusted hull and some wood decking are all that remain of the HMS *Briton*. Formerly known as the HMS *Calypso*, the ship had a long career serving in the British Navy and training Newfoundland's Royal Naval Reserve. The HMS *Briton* now rests scuttled in a small inlet near the community of Embree. The relatively well-preserved condition of the 130-year-old ship makes this site a must-see for anyone passing through the area.

HISTORY OF THE BRITON/CALYPSO

The HMS *Calypso* was built in Catham, England, in 1883. After its launch on June 7, the ship served as a third-class barque cruiser

with the British Royal Navy. The *Calypso*, with a displacement of 2,770 tons, was 71.6 metres long and 13.6 metres wide. Constructed of wood and steel, the Calypso was powered by six coal boilers, which produced 4,023 horsepower. A full set of studding sails gave it the significance of being one of the last British sailing corvettes built.

The *Calypso* served in the British Navy until September 1902, when Commander Fredrick M. Walker of Newfoundland's Royal Naval Reserve commissioned it as a training vessel and brought it to St. John's in October. The *Calypso* then served as a training vessel to instruct reservists in naval warfare techniques, allowing Newfoundland to participate in the defence of the British Empire as many other British colonies were doing at the time.

By the time the *Calypso* reached Newfoundland in October 1902, it was deemed unseaworthy and was permanently docked at the west end of St. John's Harbour. The mast, boilers, and smokestacks were dismantled and scrapped. In 1916, the ship's name was changed to HMS *Briton* and it continued to train Royal Naval Reserve service personnel until they were disbanded in 1919.

The ship remained moored to St. John's Harbour dock until 1922, when the Newfoundland government sold it to A.H. Murray Ltd. for use as a salt and coal storage barge for the city of St. John's. Thirty years later, having fallen into disrepair, the ship was towed to Lewisporte to await a decision on its future. There the ship remained tied to the dock until 1968, when it was towed to Jobs Cove near Embree, set on fire, and sunk. But the shallow cove meant that the ship did not sink far below the waterline, leaving the view seen today.

ABOUT THE AREA

Today the *Briton* rests just 50 metres from the shore. The deteriorated, rusted hull contrasts with the beauty of Indian Arm, making for unusual photo opportunities. While the ship has greatly deteriorated, most of the metal structure and wooden deck are still intact. On the south side of the *Briton* lies the deteriorated hull of the *Zarbora*, an old fishing trawler that was also purposely scuttled.

The *Briton* shipwreck is one of the most accessible wreck sites on the island. A well-travelled gravel road and a wharf stretching out near the ship ensure that visitors can get quite close.

Before the ship was scuttled, most of its equipment and parts were scrapped, donated, or placed in museums:

- The anchor is located outside Brittany Inns in Lewisporte.
- The ship's wheel and a memorial are placed in the second-floor lobby of the Surgeon Lieutenant-Commander W. Anthony Paddon Building on the north side of Quidi Vidi Lake.
- In the lobby of the HMCS Cabot on the south side of St. John's Harbour are several artifacts belonging to the *Calypso/Briton*, the most significant of which is the original Hotchkiss 3-pound, quick-firing gun.
- Another of its guns is on display at the Grand Falls Royal Canadian Legion.

Embree is a gem tucked away in the mountains of Central Newfoundland. The flat river valley where the community once was and adjacent mountains make this one of the prettiest places to visit in the area.

HMS CALYPSO/BRITON: N 49.294818, W 55.018703

From Lewisporte, travel north on Route 342 for approximately 5 kilometres. Turn onto Alex Lane and continue for approximately 300 metres on the gravel road to the shipwreck.

Andrew
+
Sava

2. Horwood Lumber Company Mill

Campbellton, Indian Arm, Notre Dame Bay

Located off Route 340 in the small community of Campbellton are the remnants of the Horwood Lumber Company Mill and the hydropower dam which powered it. The mill, built in 1913 when the forestry potential in Newfoundland was still being discovered, was a major feat for the small community and, for the few years it was in operation, it provided a greatly needed economic boost.

Today, the powerhouse, wood grinders, concrete penstocks, and dam are still visible.

HISTORY

The early 20th century brought an explosion in the Newfoundland forestry industry. Many communities already relied heavily on local sawmills but increased prices in pulp and paper meant that larger and more complex mills were needed. After an increase in the price of pulp in Canadian and American markets, in 1911 the Horwood Lumber Company chose the community of Campbellton as the location of a large pulp mill because of its proximity to the ocean and nearby Lewisporte, which provided access to the Newfoundland Railway.

The company already owned several sawmills in the area and had 370 square kilometres in timber licences for the area. The company also obtained a hydro lease for Indian Arm Brook to construct a hydroelectric dam to power the mill. The mill officially opened in the summer of 1914 and began shipping its pulp to New York for transport to other US markets.

In the spring of 1915, disaster struck when the dam upstream of

the mill was breached. The mill was forced to shut down but, with the price of pulp still high, the company decided it was worthwhile to fix the dam. Minor repairs were completed over the summer but the following spring the dam broke once again. Unfortunately, the price of pulp had fallen and the Horwood Lumber Company began experiencing financial problems. With only a small amount of pulp produced in almost four years of investment, the company decided to permanently close the mill. Many workers moved on to work in other mills, specifically the larger mill that was being constructed in nearby Glovertown.

ABOUT THE AREA

Powerhouse & Mill

Today the powerhouse is the only building left standing. It was built with reinforced concrete walls and structural supports and

would have had a roof made from wooden slabs. Connected to the powerhouse was a large 100-metre-long, 3-metre-wide circular penstock that directed water into a large room where it would spin two turbines. The turbines were directly connected to three grinders in the mill next door by a steel shaft, which remains there today. The turbines were also capable of producing electricity for company houses and the nearby sawmill.

The mill's grinders remain on the foundation of the old mill. Wood logs were fed through the small square opening, forcing it into a spinning grinder that shredded the logs into small wood chips.

The Dam & Channel

To get water to the powerhouse, a dam of approximately 350 metres long and 8 metres high was built across Indian Arm Brook. It redirected water to the east side of the reservoir where it was forced down a man-made channel before entering a penstock. The 350-metre-long channel was carved into the rock by explosives and manual labour. It ranges from 5 to 6 metres wide and up to about 7 metres deep. Along with the rock channel, concrete retaining walls up to 75 metres long and 5 metres high were constructed to contain the flow of water. The water flowed down the channel and entered the intake, where it was forced through a 3-metre-wide penstock. The concrete penstocks remain intact today.

Miniature Locomotive

Another feature is the remains of a miniature locomotive that transported pulp loads onto the wharf and into the ships. The

schooner *Nancy Lee* was often tied up to the wharf, as it was built specifically for transporting pulp from this mill to New York state.

MILL: N 49.279191, W 54.922356
DAM: N 49.276088, W 54.922274

The mill is located immediately off Route 340 in the middle of Campbellton. A dirt road on the south side of the highway leads to the trailhead (N 49.278088, W 54.921148) for a 300-metre-long trail to the dam. The trail is the old intake channel.

3.   SS *Ahern Trader* Shipwreck

Frederickton, Gander Bay

The SS *Ahern Trader* is a reminder of just how unforgiving Newfoundland and Labrador's weather can be. In 1960, while the ship was attempting to find a safe location to anchor for the night, a fierce winter storm and quickly moving sea ice caused it to run aground near the community of Frederickton. In spite of multiple salvage attempts, the ship never sailed again.

Many have argued that this wreck has become an eyesore. However, just as many have fully accepted the wreck as a piece of history and an icon of the communities nearby.

HISTORY

Launched in Scotland in 1922, the 61-metre-long, 744-tonne steel-hulled *Ahern Trader* began its career as a coastal supply vessel delivering goods to the British Isles. It sailed under the names *Lurcher*, *Ulster Coast*, and *Scottish Coast*. It was eventually purchased by the Ahern Trading Company and renamed *Ahern Trader*.

On the morning of January 8, 1960, the *Ahern Trader* arrived in Frederickton with a shipment of hay. It was on its last journey to the north coast while under charter with the Canadian National Railway. The ship docked, unloaded its cargo, and prepared to set sail again.

However, as the ship prepared to leave, a strong winter storm hit the community. Heavy winds pushed the ship into the wharf and, out of fear of damage, the captain decided to set sail and anchor farther offshore until the storm had passed. The ship exited the harbour safely and anchored to wait out the storm. Disaster struck when the winds broke the ship's chain and grounded the ship on the rocky shore.

The ship's crew blew the whistle and launched emergency flares to signal for help. According to the *Gander Beacon*, many of the residents were attending a church service when they heard the distress horn. They quickly ran to the shore to offer assistance. Thanks to the effort made by residents and the quick actions of the ship's crew, there were no injuries or loss of life.

The captain, first mate, and chief engineer stayed in Frederickton until March to oversee salvage operations. Several tugboats were brought in from St. John's to pull the ship off the rocks, but after at least four unsuccessful attempts and $70,000 in rescue operations, the ship was left aground on the rocks.

ABOUT THE LOCATION

Over the years, the rough sea has taken a toll on the ship and, section by section, it has broken apart. In 2011, after decades of standing upright, the ship toppled onto its side, its bow sticking out of the water.

The easy accessibility of the shipwreck makes it a popular stop for anyone in the Gander Bay or Musgrave Harbour area.

SS AHERN TRADER: N 49.431259, W 54.356522

Following Route 330 (Road to the Shore), turn onto Route 332, which brings you to Frederickton. Turn toward Shipwreck Point on the west side of the community's small harbour and located across from Hancott's Lane. Follow the road to its end.

4. Sir Frederick Banting's Plane Crash

Musgrave Harbour, North Coast

Encountering plane crash wreckage is always a moving experience. While every crash carries a sad tale, in February 1941 one plane crash claimed the life of a hero: Sir Frederick Grant Banting.

Frederick Banting was born in Alliston, Ontario, on November 14, 1891. After graduating from medical school, he enrolled in the military and served as part of the 13th Canadian Field Ambulance during World War I. He was awarded the Military Cross for his bravery on the battlefield, when he was injured attending wounded soldiers. Soon afterward, Banting left the military and returned to Toronto.

In 1920, Banting became a part-time teaching assistant in Physiology at the University of Western Ontario and, on October 31, 1920, it is said he woke up with an idea of how to isolate

insulin after reading medical articles about the pancreas. Over the following year, Banting and John James Rickard Macleod researched isolating insulin before successfully doing so on September 27, 1921. This discovery revolutionized the treatment of diabetes and has saved countless lives.

As a result of this discovery, on October 25, 1923, Banting and Macleod were awarded a Nobel Prize in Medicine, making Banting the first Canadian recipient of the prize. Later, in 1934, Banting was knighted by King George V.

In 1941, Banting planned to travel to London to a demonstration of a revolutionary flying suit that he had helped design that would stop pilots from passing out while completing high-speed manoeuvres. On February 20, Banting took off from Gander International Airport in a Lockheed Hudson Bomber. Shortly after takeoff, the plane experienced engine trouble, and crash-landed in a bog 16 kilometres south of Musgrave Harbour. Although the operator and the navigator died on impact, Banting and his pilot, J.C. Mackey, survived the crash. Banting, who had suffered serious injuries in the crash, died the following morning.

Today a memorial is set up in Banting Memorial Municipal Park, where an interpretation centre, a full-size replica of the doomed plane, and the remaining remnants of the crashed aircraft are visible.

BANTING'S PLANE CRASH: N 49.417899, W 53.881910
The site is located in Banting Memorial Municipal Park, approximately 4 kilometres east of the community of Musgrave Harbour on Route 330.

5. Sleepy Cove Mine
Sleepy Cove, Twillingate

Sleepy Cove was once a major industrial centre. The copper mine is another reminder of the many mines that once littered the small communities of the North Shore and, while little remains today, the area's rugged coastline provides all visitors with the incredible scenery for which the Twillingate area is renowned.

The copper mine was operated by the Great Northern Copper Company, which prospected the area between 1907 and 1917. After confirming the high-grade ore located beneath a head of land at Sleepy Cove, open-pit mining began, which soon led the company to excavate a 35-metre-deep shaft into the cliffside. At the same time, a 49-metre open cut was made in the rock, which is clearly visible. Mining operations peaked in 1918; copper prices plummeted and the mine shut down in 1920. Several prospecting expeditions and geologic investigations have been completed since then, but there has been no further mining operation.

Sleepy Cove has been transformed into a small municipal park. Many pieces of equipment belonging to the mine remain there, each telling the tale of the short-lived mine and its effect on the surrounding communities. Sleepy Cove also offers some of the best hiking and iceberg viewing in the Twillingate area.

SLEEPY COVE MINE: N 49.684855, W 54.807899

Take Route 340 north of Twillingate. About 600 metres past the community of Mutford's Cove, turn left onto a small gravel road. The mine and municipal park are at the end of the short road.

6. *Miss Bayview II & South Twillingate Island Ferry Terminal*

Black Duck Cove, South Twillingate Island

Rising out of the water near the tiny community of Black Duck Cove on South Twillingate Island is the wreck of the *Miss Bayview II*. The fishing vessel, built by A.F. Theriault & Son Ltd. in Meteghan River, Nova Scotia, in 1964, was christened the *Lady Yvette* but renamed *Miss Bayview II* in 1998. The ship measured 29 metres long and 7.5 metres wide and had a gross tonnage of 188 tons. For the first part of the ship's life, it was used as a scallop dragger before transporting cargo along the coast of Newfoundland and Labrador. As the ship aged, its use as an ocean-going vessel diminished. Eventually, it was tied to the old South Twillingate Island ferry dock and left exposed to the harsh weather, sea, and ice conditions.

Located next to the ship are the remains of the ferry terminal, once the primary transportation route between New World Island and South Twillingate Island. In 1973, a bridge was built over the Main Tickle between the islands and ferry service ceased.

MISS BAYVIEW II: N 49.596404, W 54.703841

On Route 340 toward Twillingate, pass the Main Tickle bridge, enter South Twillingate Island, and turn onto Black Duck Cove Road (located behind the Prime Berth Fishing Museum). Follow the road to its end to the dock and shipwreck.

7. Lower Little Harbour Sea Arch

Little Harbour, South Twillingate Island

It's a big arch in a little harbour. The 10-metre-high Lower Little Harbour sea arch, located south of Twillingate, was carved from thousands of years of wave and ice erosion along the exposed northern coast. This natural sea arch is rare: you can walk through it during low-water levels and also experience it from above, by hiking over the top of the arch. Exercise caution, as the low vegetation and loose rocks close to the coast can be dangerous. But the arch, one of the more impressive in the area, is worth the visit.

On the way to the arch, you pass through the abandoned fields and root cellars of a resettled community. In summer, the hike offers chances to spot icebergs and whales.

⊕ SEA ARCH: N 49.633782, W 54.698733

The trailhead (N 49.627655, W 54.709613) for the arch is located approximately 350 metres off Route 340 on Little Harbour Road. Parking is available along the side of the road. Follow the Lower Little Harbour Trail for approximately 1.2 kilometres at its shortest length.

NATURAL
ARCH

8. Gander Ammunition Bunkers

Gander International Airport

At the time it was constructed in 1938, Gander International Airport was the largest airport in the world and, during World War II, it was transformed into a crucial air force base for military aircraft. The airfield was much larger than it is today: it contained hundreds of buildings, hangers, and barracks. Walking along the

north side of the airport today, you see evidence of this history: straight, birch tree-lined roads, empty lots, and a few remaining building foundations make up the town of Gander's Former Townsite. But the gradual shrinking of the airport and the British, Canadian, and American air force bases that once surrounded the airfield have left a collection of artifacts behind.

Approximately half a dozen abandoned ammunition and storage bunkers are located near the still-operating Canadian Forces Base, 9 Wing Gander. The abandoned igloo-style bunkers have been converted to non-military uses such as storage for sand and gravel. The dirt-covered concrete bunkers have become overgrown. The bunkers were once accessible by a dirt road that intersects James Boulevard; a gate now prohibits large vehicles from entering the site.

 **GANDER AMMUNITION BUNKERS:** N 48.942517, W 54.593254

The bunkers are located near the modern-day Canadian Forces Base, approximately 1 kilometre on a gravel road off James Boulevard. In recent years, a gate placed across the trail prohibits entry. If you wish to explore this site, contact the base and local landowners first.

9.   The "Turkey Farm"

Gander, Central Newfoundland

While Gander International Airport today operates only a fraction of the incoming and outgoing flights it once did, it is still a common stopover and emergency landing site for the world's aircraft. Anyone who has visited the airport has probably noticed what appears to be a giant fence peeking through the treetops in the forest behind the airfield.

Known locally as the "Turkey Farm," the fencing is an enormous antennae system operated by the Canadian Air Force. The complex is made up of a system of antennas which encircle a small operations building at its centre, officially called an AN/FRD-10 system. The 34-metre-tall aluminum antennas rise above the surrounding landscape. The approximately 250-metre-diameter circle consists of outer antennas used for detecting longer, low-frequency wavelengths (2–8 MHz); the inner antennas for shorter, high-frequency wavelengths (8–30 MHz).

Built around 1970, the AN/FRD-10 system, commonly called "Wullenwebber" (the American version of the same radio system),

replaced a small World War II-era system that operated out of a nearby house. When the facility, one of the largest supplementary radio stations in the country, was established, it required 291 operators, who became known locally as Turkey Farmers.

Debate exists as to the origin of the term "Turkey Farm." One article suggests that it came from a rivalry between a similar station in British Columbia, known as the Elephant Trap. Although as of 2021 the Gander facility continues to operate, it will likely not be long before it becomes obsolete and decommissioned as many others of its kind have. For now, the "Turkey Farm" inspires stories of secret military operations and coverups.

◎ THE "TURKEY FARM": N 48.951087, W 54.525371

Heading toward the airport on James Boulevard, turn left at Garret Drive and take the first right onto Circular Road. Travel approximately 2.6 kilometres, then veer left and continue on Circular Road. A farther 1.7 kilometres bring you as close as possible to the complex.

10. Thomas Howe Demonstration Forest Crash Site

Gander

Gander's long aviation history means that the area surrounding the once-busy airport is dotted with fragments from this period in the town's history. Among them are the many crash sites and signs of aircraft wreckage throughout the forest and bogs surrounding the town. These are sometimes accompanied by stories of survival and overcoming great odds to find rescue, but many remnants carry stories of peril and despair. One such case is the wreckage of a United States Air Force aircraft in what is now the Thomas Howe Demonstration Forest.

After refuelling in Gander, the aircraft and its 10 crew members took off on December 29, 1943, en route to complete their journey from the US to Wales, UK. The aircraft, a Boeing B-17G Flying Fortress, was part of the Second Ferry Group of the Forth Ferry Squadron. Classified as a bomber, it was propelled by four 1,200-horsepower "cyclone" engines which gave it a maximum takeoff weight of almost 30,000 kilograms. The large aircraft had a wingspan of 32 metres and a length of 23 metres.

Immediately after the aircraft took off from Gander, it began to bank left as it made a turn toward the south. Witnesses say that the plane quickly lost altitude as it made the turn and, as it did, the wings made contact with the ground, causing the plane to crash and break apart, killing all on board.

The crash site is now traversed by the trails of the Thomas Howe Demonstration Forest, an outdoor facility designed to educate visitors on ecosystems and the forestry management practices of Newfoundland's forest. Along these trails, however, are many pieces of aircraft wreckage and debris. Informative signs and easy-to-walk trails make this crash site easy to access.

CRASH SITE: N 48.930795, W 54.588078

The Thomas Howe Demonstration Forest is located on the Trans-Canada Highway approximately 1.3 kilometres east of the exit to Route 330. At the end of a short gravel road, a series of marked trails go through the forest to the crash site.

New-Wes-Valley
Gander
Salvage
1
Glovertown
6
Ellis
2
3
Terra Nova
4
5
Port Blandford
7
Clarenville
8
Goobies
Swift Current
9
10
Bay L'Argent
Whitbourne
Placentia
Grand Bank
Marystown
Burin
St. Lawrence
12
11
Lamaline

East Coast

Bonavista, Clarenville, & Burin Peninsula

For the purposes of this book, the east coast of Newfoundland is defined as the east side of the main island, treating the Avalon Peninsula as its own entity. This region is made up of three very distinguishable places: the Bonavista Peninsula, the Clarenville Region, and the Burin Peninsula. While each contains its own unique history, heritage, and landscapes, they share the common characteristic of being driven by the cod fishery. Near Bonavista, Newfoundland's cod stocks were first recognized, leading to the colonization of the island a short time later. The area became a prominent fishing and merchant centre for northern Newfoundland and the towns of Bonavista and Trinity became hubs for the peninsula. Each town that dots the jagged, cliff-lined coast has preserved its heritage through its architecture, museums, and continued reliance on the fishery.

Farther south, Clarenville is a modern hub town situated along the protected bays of Smith Sound and Northwest Arm, which together surround Random Island. If you drive westward along the Trans-Canada Highway from St. John's, the Clarenville area offers the first views of the lush, birch tree forests and rolling hills that make up most of Central Newfoundland.

The Burin Peninsula is the third distinguishable area in the region. Commonly described as the boot of Newfoundland, this peninsula boasts barren and boggy landscapes. Its infamous fog did not stop fishers from settling in its hundreds of coves and harbours, however. Communities such as Marystown, Burin, and Grand Bank became prominent towns for merchants and shipbuilders. Today the region continues to thrive on the Grand Bank fishery, offshore oil support and fabrication, and mining in St. Lawrence.

The entire region contains many geologic and ecological wonders, including the Fortune Head Ecological Reserve and the Discovery Geopark (a recognized UNESCO Global Geopark).

From Clarenville and the Trans-Canada Highway, travel north

along the Discovery Trail (Route 230) to explore the Bonavista Peninsula and all of its tourism hotspots. From the town of Bonavista, Route 235 loops around the peninsula. Explore the many smaller roads that lead to the communities dotting the coast to fully experience the region—and maybe glimpse the icebergs and whales that pass through the area each year.

South of Clarenville is the community of Goobies and the start of Route 210 to the Burin Peninsula. Although several side

highways bring you to picturesque communities along the way, the drive along the main road from Goobies to Marystown/Burin is barren and desolate. Be sure to prepare for this drive, as a lack of people and the area's notorious wind, fog, and snow make the road potentially dangerous. From the town of Marystown, follow Route 220 to loop around the lower peninsula and take in some of Newfoundland's most fascinating history and landscapes.

1. Dungeon Provincial Park

Cape Bonavista

Dungeon Provincial Park is not entirely unknown but it is often overshadowed by the Bonavista Lighthouse and nearby historic town of Bonavista. The Dungeon is a collapsed sea cave which has the distinctive feature of two entrances. The hole was formed from thousands of years of erosion along the cliffside. Eventually, the 600-million-year-old sedimentary rocks eroded to form two sea caves. As the caves grew larger, they eventually joined into a tunnel before erosion caused the roof to collapse.

The enormous hole remains one of Newfoundland's geologic wonders. During the early summer, hundreds of icebergs backdrop the sea caves. The location offers another unusual hazard: cows. As you travel to the site, you pass through a cow pasture, where the friendly inhabitants often approach visitors.

DUNGEON PROVINCIAL PARK: N 48.666832, W 53.084428

As you drive along Cape Shore Drive toward Cape Bonavista, turn right onto a small gravel road named Lance Cove Road, located approximately 3.1 kilometres south of the Cape Bonavista Lighthouse. Drive 2 kilometres along the road to the destination and lookout area.

2.   Bonavista Airstrip

Little Catalina

Located just north of the community of Little Catalina, the small paved Bonavista Airstrip is almost entirely abandoned—it still has occasional recreational visitors and is equipped for emergency flights and landings. The 610-metre-long and 23-metre-wide airstrip was constructed in 1972 and operated by the provincial government. Today, due to its poor condition, it is more commonly used as a walking track for locals living nearby than as an actual airstrip.

BONAVISTA AIRSTRIP: N 48.566850, W 53.060561
Approximately 5 kilometres north of Catalina turn onto a small gravel road. Travel another 1 kilometre to arrive at the site. As the airfield is still reportedly used from time to time, caution is advised.

3. Arch Rock

Little Catalina

The gently sloped, grassy terrace that gives way to the windswept, jagged coast of Little Catalina Harbour is one place to experience the Bonavista Peninsula landscape. Within the community, the best place to get close to the rock-lined coast is via the Arch Rock Trail on the harbour's south side. This trail gets its name from an extraordinary rock located several metres from shore. The rock contains three arches, two of which cut perpendicular to shore and a third that cuts parallel. The largest of these arches allows visitors to peer through it, providing a unique view of the shoreline across the harbour.

Continue along the trail to small rocky beaches in narrow cuts in the cliff face and, in many cases, small caves and arches in early stages of formation. Look for fossils along the sloped rocks as you trek to the site.

ARCH ROCK: N 48.535931, W 53.044737

Follow Little Catalina Road into the community. Turn right onto Mars Meadow and right again onto Dayton Road. The trailhead (N 48.539591, W 53.046186) is located at the end of the short road, and parking is possible along the side of the road. Arch Rock is accessible by a boggy, 500-metre-long ATV trail that roughly follows the coastline.

4. Town of Port Union

Port Union, Bonavista Peninsula

Located off the popular Bonavista Peninsula highway, Port Union is recognized as the only union-built town in North America. Today its wooden buildings and deteriorated houses are a reminder of the revolutionary town that helped better the lives of thousands of Newfoundland fishers.

HISTORY

For most of the 19th century, Newfoundland and Labrador's economy was heavily based around the truck system, in which fishers traded their yearly catch to a local merchant in return for food and equipment. More often than not, fishers took out credit from the merchant before their fishing expeditions to acquire equipment and supplies. Because of this, merchants could set the price of goods based partly on international markets and their desired profit. At the time, merchants were the only people who knew the prices and markets and thus could take advantage of fishers and force them into greater debt.

This system continued until 1908, when St. John's-born William Ford Coaker began a social movement to unite fishers around the province into the Fishermen's Protective Union (FPU). The FPU's main objective was to aid in the sharing of information related to equipment, food, and fish prices which, in turn, would help standardize prices and provide fishers with equal work for equal pay. To do this, the FPU established its own newspaper, trading post, and community support groups.

By 1909, the FPU consisted of 50 local councils. In 1914, it had approximately 21,060 members. Although most of the union activity was based out of a small headquarters in St. John's, in order to succeed the way Coaker envisioned more space and political freedom was needed.

In 1915, Coaker purchased land rights to an area surrounding a protected harbour on the east side of the Bonavista Peninsula near the small community of Catalina. Construction began in 1916 and in early 1918 the FPU officially relocated its headquarters to Port Union.

Over the next 50 years, it became a prominent international trading post and industrialized town consisting of:

- Salt fish processing plant, department store, seal oil plant, and machine shop
- Shipyard owned by the FPU's Union Shipbuilding Company
- Two rows of wooden duplexes which housed the town's employees
- Customs office, making the port internationally recognized
- Hydroelectric dam to provide power for the town
- Hotel, bakery, and a soft drink manufacturing plant

- Convention centre, which, before burning down in 1945, was described as being bright enough to see from far out at sea and acted as a beacon for fishers

Much of the town burned down in 1945, but was quickly reconstructed. By the 1950s, Port Union was one of the largest exporters of salt cod on the east coast.

The FPU's activity declined during the 1980s and 1990s, changing politics, economy, and the 1992 moratorium on northern cod. After the moratorium, the major employer, the Fishery Products fish plant, was forced to shut down due to fish shortages.

Although the town was slowly abandoned, in 1998 the Port Union historic industrial district was nationally recognized as a National Historic Site, helping preserve the history of the town.

ABOUT THE AREA

After most of the industrial and historic parts were left vacant, the Town of Port Union and the William F. Coaker Foundation restored the town's buildings. Many of the restored buildings, including the factory and William Coaker's house (known as "The Bungalow"), are now open for tours and visits. In other parts of the town, rows of houses and buildings remain abandoned and deteriorating. The town, a fragment of its former self, is still a worthwhile place to visit.

 **PORT UNION:** N 48.498652, W 53.081406

Port Union is located along Highway 230. The historic district is located along the south side of the harbour, with its core along Main Road near the waterfront.

5.   The Trinity Loop

Trinity, Bonavista Peninsula

The Trinity Loop is Newfoundland's own abandoned theme park. Constructed in 1910, the loop was originally designed to allow trains travelling on the Newfoundland Railway to access the community of Trinity by allowing them to slowly descend into the coastal town. After the Newfoundland Railway closed in 1984, the loop was turned into an amusement park.

HISTORY

For over 90 years, the Newfoundland Railway was a vital transportation network. The main railway line ran from St. John's to Port aux Basques; smaller branch lines connected the main line to many rural communities around the province. In November 1911, the owners of the Newfoundland Railway, the Reid Newfoundland Company, opened a branch line on the Bonavista Peninsula. This railway line was generally easy to construct because of the peninsula's small topographic changes.

One problem arose, however, when they attempted to bring the railway line through the town of Trinity. Its location along the coast, surrounded by steep hills, made it difficult for trains to descend. The solution: a 2-kilometre extension that looped around a small pond (later named Loop Pond) to gradually lower the elevation of the railway tracks. The Reid Newfoundland Company hired engineer J.P. Powell to design the extension.

In Powell's system, the incoming tracks in the northwest crossed over a small river valley, circled around Loop Pond, and then passed under itself before continuing through the valley

BY
SHS

into the community. The design was similar to loops in mountain passes in western Canada.

Construction of the loop began in 1910 and finished the following year. The 2-kilometre, 310-degree loop decreases the track's elevation by 10.3 metres. The loop continued operation until 1984, when railway owner Terra Transport Company closed it down.

At the time, the original plan was to scrap this section of the railway line, but retired railway worker and local historian Clayton Cook organized campaigns and petitions to save the unique feature. With the help of several politicians, the Terra Transport Company agreed to transfer ownership of the loop to the town of Trinity.

Francis Kelly purchased the land and turned it into an amusement park, preserving the railway loop and bridge. This park included boat rides, accommodations, amusement rides, a museum, and a train ride around the loop. In February 1988, the Trinity Loop was registered as a heritage structure. The park operated successfully for several years but, but due to declining interest, in 2004 it was shut down.

ABOUT THE LOCATION

Today the park is in ruins. In September 2010, Hurricane Igor devastated the Trinity Loop. Extensive rainfall caused the river flowing through the park to wash away 100 feet of track and deposit rocks and sediment over the remaining rides and features.

The most striking feature of the park is the Ferris wheel, which now lies on the ground. Other former rides and a mini-golf course are still visible, but the most intact features are the train engines, passenger cars, and overgrown railway line. Despite its poor condition, the park serves as a reminder of the Newfoundland Railway and the built heritage of the province.

THE TRINITY LOOP: N 48.365687, W 53.397736

From Route 230 to Bonavista, turn onto Route 239 (Main Road) into Trinity. The access road to the Trinity Loop is located 3.5 kilometres along this road, across from the Canada Post Office. Turn onto the paved but unmaintained road and travel another 1.6 kilometres to the Trinity Loop.

And I caught sight of a woman sitting
a scarlet-coloured wild beast that was full
and that had seven heads and ten horns.
was arrayed in purple and scarlet, and
gold and precious
cup that was full of disgusting things and
fornication. And upon her forehead was written
"Babylon the Great, the mother of the

6. Terra Nova Sulphite Company Pulp Mill

Glovertown

One of the largest abandoned buildings in Newfoundland and Labrador is the Terra Nova Sulphite Company Pulp Mill in Glovertown. This large concrete structure towers over the banks of the Terra Nova River.

The mill once promised to bring jobs and benefits to the people of Glovertown, but due to financial difficulties and the mill's inadequate size, owners and investors shut it down before it began operating.

HISTORY

During the early 20th century, the construction of the Newfoundland Railway resulted in better accessibility to the interior of the island, opening up Central Newfoundland's forestry industry. After recognizing the success in nearby Grand Falls, the Terra Nova Sulphite Company, with the aid of Norwegian investors, began constructing a pulp mill on the banks of the Terra Nova River. The location was ideal because of its proximity to a saltwater port and shipping routes and because it was on a large river that could be used to supply power to the mill.

In early 1921, the Newfoundland government granted the company timber rights for the area surrounding the Terra Nova River and the rights for the construction of a hydro dam. Construction began soon after, with an expected completion date in the spring of 1922. The first phase was the construction of a wharf at Angle Brook (later amalgamated into the community of Glovertown), and with a high expectation for success, businesses, schools, worker housing, and a medical centre were built before the mill was completed.

In the fall of 1922, however, work on the mill was halted when the Norwegian investors fell into financial trouble because of a decline in the Norwegian currency. The Newfoundland government became skeptical of the investor's commitment and it refused to provide the loans requested by the owners to finish the project.

In 1923, the owners of the highly successful Grand Falls Pulp and Paper Mill, the Anglo-Newfoundland Development Company (AND Company), bought the nearly completed mill and its timber rights for about $2 million. AND then sent 1,300 cords of cut wood to the mill to test its capabilities. Although the tests were successful, the AND Company decided that the mill was too small to be profitable.

Citizens from Glovertown who waited in anticipation for the mill to boost the local economy protested the decision. Letters and petitions were sent to both the AND Company and the Newfoundland government, but it was not enough.

After the mill was shut down, most of the removable material, machinery, and equipment were dismantled and shipped to mills in Bishop's Falls and Grand Falls. But the concrete structure of the building and dam on the Terra Nova River were untouched.

ABOUT THE AREA

Today the 35-metre-tall, 125-metre-long building towers in the forest behind Glovertown. Although the structure is in relatively good shape, signs warn of falling debris; its height makes falling debris a definite hazard. The remains of a small dam are also visible on the Terra Nova River next to the mill.

In 2020, Glovertown mayor Doug Churchill and the town council recognized the heritage and tourism benefits of these abandoned structures. A fence has been placed around the structure. But, looking to capitalize and promote the province's built heritage, the town is attempting to make the site a recognized attraction, with an informative walking trail encircling the building.

⊕ TERRA NOVA SULPHITE COMPANY PULP MILL:
N 48.665811, W 54.011070

The easily accessible pulp mill is located at the end of Angle Brook Road in Glovertown, which intersects Main Street (aka Route 310). After 600 metres, Angle Brook Road turns to gravel; continue another 250 metres to the destination.

7. Burgoynes Cove B-36 Crash
Burgoynes Cove, Trinity Bay

On the night of March 17, 1953, General Richard E. Ellsworth and his crew took off from the Canary Islands on a mission to test North American air defences. The mission took a tragic turn when a change in weather conditions pushed the plane off course, causing the enormous B-36 Peacemaker to crash into a mountain on the western side of Trinity Bay, killing all 23 crew members.

Today, the wreckage rests on a hilltop near the community of Burgoynes Cove, east of Clarenville. The debris field is enormous and, while it is difficult to piece together most of the aircraft, sections of the fuselage, tail wing, and engines are distinguishable. The crash site not only offers dramatic views of the surrounding area but survives as a tribute to the servicemen who lost their lives.

In 1953, the Cold War between the US and the Soviet Union was just beginning and in order to test North American defence systems, a squadron of 18 RB-36H reconnaissance aircraft from the 28th Reconnaissance Wing prepared to take off from the Canary Islands to fly into the US undetected. The planes were set to fly at a 500-foot altitude to avoid radar detection; once they entered the continental US, they would ascend to 40,000 feet and proceed to their designated "targets."

On the night of March 17, 1953, the squadron took off in 15-minute intervals en route to Maine. Mission commander General Richard E. Ellsworth and his 22 crew members in the first plane to leave were the only people in the operation to know when the mission would begin. To navigate to the US in total secrecy, the pilots would rely on simple navigation techniques such as sextants and star navigation and on weather forecasts predicted before their departure. This meant that the aircraft would be flying without the aid of any modern technology.

Ellsworth's aircraft began its career as a B-36D Peacemaker designed to drop bombs on Nazi Germany during World War II. Six 3,800-horsepower engines and four General Electric turbojet engines added to the size of the aircraft but meant that it could travel at faster speeds and for longer distances. For its final mission, the aircraft was fitted to carry a specialized camera and reconnaissance equipment.

Ellsworth and his crew were aware of the deteriorating weather conditions that were expected over their 23-hour mission but continual cloud cover prohibited the use of sextants to determine if they were following the correct route. An unexpected change in

a low-pressure system they were flying through caused the plane to be pushed northward more than expected.

Early in the morning of March 18, the aircraft did not come ashore in Maine as planned, but in Trinity Bay. It was flying low as instructed and, as a result, hit the barren hilltop of Burgoynes Cove, causing the plane to disintegrate upon impact. All 23 on board died almost immediately.

Residents of nearby communities were just waking up when they heard the explosion and saw smoke. A rescue party was quickly formed and hiked through deep snow for almost 2 hours to reach the summit and crash site, but little could be done. The crash had left a 75-metre-wide debris field; the aircraft's fuselage and wings were completely mangled; and small fires burned around the site. It soon became clear that no one had survived.

The rescue party made its way to a small community on

Random Island and telephoned the RCMP in Clarenville. Word soon reached the Canadian Air Force base in Gander, which sent two planes to the site. Medics parachuted down and were updated on the situation by the first responders.

A clearing was cut to allow a US Coast Guard helicopter to land to retrieve the bodies. It transported the bodies to the nearby community of Monroe, where they were moved onto a US Coast Guard seaplane and brought to Torbay Airport. From there, hearses transported the fallen soldiers to the American base at Fort Pepperrell in St. John's.

This was not the only disaster to happen on this day. After Ellsworth and his crew did not arrive with the rest of the

squadron in Maine, a B-29 Superfortress of the 52nd Air Rescue Squadron out of Harmon Air Force Base in Stephenville was sent to locate the aircraft. After an unsuccessful search, the aircraft turned back toward Harmon Air Force Base. Before it could reach its destination, it and its 10 crew members disappeared. It was never found; the cause and location of this crash remain unknown.

ABOUT THE AREA

The crash site is located on the hills overlooking Random Island. As you approach the summit of the hill, you will see pieces of the aircraft scattered through the forest. The scale of the disaster becomes apparent at the top. In a small rock-cut gully, thousands of pieces of bent metal and fuselage lie piled up. Pieces of the wing and engines are recognizable and the tail section remains relatively intact. A plaque memorializing the men who died there was erected on August 3, 1993, by the 103rd RU Flight Engineering command.

CRASH SITE: N 48.184070, W 53.663554

As you drive into the community of Burgoynes Cove on Route 232, turn left onto a small paved road (N 48.171020, W 53.716209) heading north. Travel along this road, staying right at any intersections, for approximately 5.2 kilometres. The trailhead is located on the left (N 48.177699, W 53.665306). The crash is located at the end of a 1.1-kilometre-long hiking trail that can be relatively steep in sections.

8. Black Brook Falls

North West River, Southwest Arm

As you travel east on the Trans-Canada Highway and descend the winding roads into Southwest Arm and the community of North West Brook, you cross Black Brook bridge. There, on your left, a brook flows down from the mountains before going under the bridge and disappearing—it actually plunges over 15 metres into a narrow gorge adjacent to the bridge. The hidden waterfall marks the beginning of numerous waterfalls throughout the hilly region. This one, like many, is difficult to find and even more difficult to access. Nestled among the thick forest and dramatic topographic changes in the area, it requires a steep hike through the woods to witness it from below.

BLACK BROOK FALLS: N 48.020390, W 53.962349

Access the community of North West Brook via the exit to Route 204 toward Hodge's Cove and Little Heart's Ease. Travel 1.6 kilometres, turn left onto Harbour Drive, then left again onto Black Brook Drive. Follow the road for approximately 900 metres to a cul-de-sac, where parking is available. A final 200-metre-long difficult hike is required down the thick, forested hill to see the falls.

9. Newfoundland's First Pulp Mill

North West River, Southwest Arm

Typically, when we think of Newfoundland's built heritage, we often think of saltbox houses, Cabot Tower, or the province's historic lighthouses. But this is not always the case, and nowhere demonstrates this better than the remnants of the Black River Pulp Mill: Newfoundland's first pulp mill.

Today not much remains of the mill. Concrete foundations, steel grinders, and other pieces of equipment lie in the grown-over field where the mill was once located. But the area's historical significance mixed with the scenery of Placentia Bay makes it worth visiting for anyone travelling down the Burin Peninsula Highway (Route 210).

HISTORY

The Black River Pulp Mill, built in 1897 by the Newfoundland Chemical Wood Pulp Company, was owned by Harvey and Company, a St. John's business that hoped to attract British investors and British paper mills to exploit the forestry potential of the island.

In an attempt to spark interest, the company built a "trial" pulp mill at the mouth of Black River, near the community of Swift Current. This site was ideal: it was on a major river, which could generate power and its proximity to a deep, ice-free saltwater bay allowed easy shipping of materials and goods. Construction began in May 1897 and was completed in November of the same year. Four hundred workers were hired to build a dam, mill, offices, stores, and a manager's residence.

To operate the mill, water flowing over the top of the adjacent dam spun several turbines, providing power. The turbines could generate up to 12,000 horsepower at peak flow, allowing the mill to produce up to 20 tons of pulp every day.

Pulp production began immediately. Forty people were hired to work in the mill and another 200 to log the surrounding area. These loggers harvested 340 square kilometres of forest purchased by the company near Pipers Hole River. In February 1898, 2,000 tons of pulp were shipped to Manchester, England, where it was distributed to several paper mills and investors around the country.

Although the quality of the pulp was high, investors showed little interest in the product and did not think the operation was of adequate size or design to be a viable investment. Most investors believed that insufficient water levels on the river and the high operating cost of the mill would prevent the venture from becoming profitable. Because of this, the Newfoundland Chemical Wood Pulp Company was forced to shut down in 1903, six years after being constructed.

The Black River Pulp Mill's failure left many investors and local business owners with the impression that pulp mills in Newfoundland would not be profitable, and its pulp and paper industry looked bleak. However, over the last 100 years, pulp mills have become a valuable asset to Newfoundland's economy—and it all began with the Black River Pulp Mill.

ABOUT THE AREA

Among the overgrown trees and grass on the shore of Placentia Bay lie the concrete foundations, wood grinders, and remnants of the rock-lined dam. The concrete structure sits over a small tunnel filled with sea water. Water redirected by the dam once flowed through this tunnel and powered the mill's turbines and grinder. Throughout the area are many more concrete foundations and rusting machinery that once were part of this mill.

This area is a sobering reminder of what happens when an important part of Newfoundland's history is neglected. No plaque or memorial marks the location and, except for local websites and brief references in books, the Black River Pulp Mill has been lost to time.

PULP MILL: N 47.879757, W 54.168634

From the Trans-Canada Highway at Goobies, travel 17.3 kilometres on Route 210. Turn left onto a paved road to Garden Cove and travel a further 1.5 kilometres. Leaving from the trailhead (N 47.880076, W 54.167233), walk 100 metres to the mouth of the river where the mill was located.

10. The Wreck of *Senator Penny*

Little Harbour East, Fortune Bay

Rising above the waterline of Fortune Bay is the steel superstructure of the fishing trawler *Senator Penny*, built to join the otter trawl fleet owned by John Penny and Sons of Ramea. Constructed in the W.C. McKay Shipyard in Shelbourne, Nova Scotia, it was launched in 1959. It was towed to Lunenburg, where its engine, equipment, and rigging were installed, and then arrived at Ramea on February 6, 1960. The ship was likely named for George Penny, one of the first Newfoundlanders to be part of the Canadian Senate and husband of Marie (Smart) Penny, who owned John Penny and Sons.

For most of its life, the *Senator Penny* operated along the south coast of Newfoundland. It would leave its berth in Ramea, pick up its crew from nearby communities, travel to the Grand Banks, and catch haddock. The ship was used as a trawler until 1982, when it became a passenger ferry servicing the Burgeo-Ramea-Grey River route and a mobile clinic in the isolated community of Grey River. Over time, the demand for a car-carrying ship increased and the *Senator Penny* was replaced. John Penny and Sons beached the ship just north of the Fortune Bay community of Little Harbour East.

Much of the hull has slipped below the water but the super-structure peeks out of the water.

⊕ THE *SENATOR PENNY*: N 47.568607, W 54.843037
Travel 4.5 kilometres north of Little Bay East along Route 212 to the trailhead (N 47.573964, W 54.837968). Follow rough ATV trails until you have to venture through the woods to the seaside.

11. St. Lawrence Fluorspar Mines
St. Lawrence, Burin Peninsula

The St. Lawrence Fluorspar Mines, operated since the late 1930s, remain a major employer on the Burin Peninsula. The mining operation observed while travelling on Route 220 is the most recent of many mines that extract the fluorspar-rich rocks used in such products as aluminum and glass.

Throughout the region are signs of mining operations. Near the start of the Chambers Cove hiking trail are the Iron Spring mine remains. Clearly marked, this site was the first fluorspar deposit to be discovered and mined in the early 1930s. Long sealed shut, the shaft and concrete foundations remain in the overgrown, boggy landscape. Currently registered as a municipal heritage site for the importance of its discovery, it was one of

the most productive fluorspar mines in the world. In nearby Blue Beach Cove, another large concrete structure is overgrown and slowly falling apart.

After being closed for nearly 40 years, the fluorspar mines recently resumed operations. The history of the mines is indelibly etched in the town of St. Lawrence, which has both prospered and suffered deeply. Many mine workers developed silicosis and lung cancer, casting a tragic shadow over the mine's success.

⊕ FLUORSPAR MINES: N 46.885764, W 55.416559
In St. Lawrence, turn off Route 220 onto Laurentian Avenue. Travel 1.7 kilometres, turn onto Pollux Avenue, and travel 3.4 kilometres on the mostly gravel road to the Iron Springs mine. Stay clear of current mining operations.

12. Chambers Cove

St. Lawrence, Burin Peninsula

Newfoundland is no stranger to shipwrecks and disasters at sea. But to the people of St. Lawrence and Little St. Lawrence, no disaster is closer to home than that at Chambers Cove. And few other disaster stories better demonstrate the resilience and kind-heartedness of Newfoundlanders.

In the early morning of February 18, 1942, three American navy ships were travelling through heavy seas and low visibility

toward the naval base at Argentia. Off course and unable to obtain a position so early in the morning, the destroyer warships USS *Wilkes* and USS *Truxtun*, along with the accompanying supply ship USS *Pollux*, ran aground along the steep coastal cliffs at Lawn Head, Chambers Cove, and Lawn Point, respectively. The *Wilkes* managed to escape the rocks, but the heavy seas and strong winds prevented any escape by the *Pollux* or *Truxtun*. The sailors struggled for hours, attempting to reach the shore to climb the steep cliffs of the exposed cove. Finally, a few made it ashore and managed to get to the nearby St. Lawrence Fluorspar Mines for help. Mine workers and the townspeople of nearby St. Lawrence quickly trekked through the thick forest to rescue the remaining crew of the ships, risking their own lives by climbing down the steep hillside during the winter storm. In all, 186 service personnel were rescued, but over 203 perished.

A memorial and guided trail now share the story of that fateful night, the sailors involved, and those who saved as many as they could. The ships did not remain above water long before they were pulled below the surface. Today, the only way to see these ships is by diving—but that does not mean that the disaster will soon be forgotten.

CHAMBERS COVE: N 46.877793, W 55.433134

In St. Lawrence, turn off Route 220 onto Laurentian Avenue. Travel 1.7 kilometres, turn onto Pollux Avenue, and travel 3.8 kilometres on the mostly gravel road before arriving at a parking area and trailhead (N 46.884117, W 55.420163). From here, an easy 1.5-kilometre-long well-maintained trail guides you to the cove.

Grates C
Old Perlican
Northern Bay
9
8
7
New Perlican
Broad Cove
Heart's Content
Sunnyside
Carbonear
5
Harbour Grace
6
4
Chance Cove
12
10
Thornlea
11
13
Dildo
3
Brigus
2
1
Colliers
Whitbourne
Holyrood
Colinet

Trinity Bay & Conception Bay West

This area is full of pirate stories, some of the island's oldest permanent European settlements, and former Beothuk fishing and hunting grounds. Receding glaciers carved up the landscape and left much of it barren, but people have settled in every nook and cranny of the jagged coastlines of Conception and Trinity Bays.

Evidence suggests that the Beothuk fished and hunted along the western side of the isthmus connecting the Avalon Peninsula to the rest of the island. Much later, the first modern European colony was established in Cuper's Cove (now Cupids) in 1610. While this did lead to the permanent presence of Europeans on the island, the colony itself was short-lived because of unforgiving weather conditions. The region would go on to contain some of the largest communities of the 18th and 19th centuries. Harbour Grace, Carbonear, and Heart's Delight soon became merchant hubs hosting English and Irish immigrants, whose stonework created impressive churches and other buildings.

Sealing, fishing, and Arctic exploration helped develop the region. Brigus, home of renowned explorer Bob Bartlett, remains a picture-perfect town, known for its lush gardens and prominent houses. The sheltered harbours that protected those who lived in them also preserved several shipwrecks, which are still visible.

The Trans-Canada Highway is the base for travel east and west across the region. In the west, Route 201 travels along the coastline of southern Trinity Bay, reaching the communities of Chance Cove, Bellevue, and Chapel Arm. But most of the region can best be seen by travelling Routes 80 and 70, a loop which allows visitors to be in both Conception and Trinity Bays—and the chance to see icebergs and whales in summer.

1. SS *Charcot*, SS *Southern Foam*, & SS *Sukha*

Conception Harbour, Conception Bay

Rising from the waters of Conception Bay is the rusted hull of the SS *Charcot*. The shipwreck was long a local secret, but recently its location just minutes off the Conception Bay Highway, has made it a must-see. But there's more: located immediately behind the wreck, and just a few metres below the surface of the water, are the remains of the SS *Southern Foam* and the SS *Sukha*. These ships met an unfortunate end over 50 years ago after they broke free from a

nearby wharf and grounded in the small cove. They remain a lasting reminder of Newfoundland's connection to the sea.

HISTORY

The *Charcot* was built in 1923 for A/S Hvalen in Tonsberg, Norway. Named after polar explorer Dr. Jean Baptiste Charcot, the ship was a whaling ship for most of its career, except when it operated as a patrol ship in the Royal Navy during World War II. With a length of 35.6 metres and a width of 6.6 metres, this steel-hulled ship was powered by a 609-horsepower coal/oil boiler, ideal for withstanding the waves and sea ice of northern Newfoundland.

In 1943, the ship was sold to the Polar Whaling Company and operated out of a whaling station in Hawke Harbour, Labrador. It was sold again in 1956 to the Hawke Harbour Whaling Company, until the whaling station burned down and the ship was moved to Conception Harbour, where it remained tied up for the next decade.

During a storm in 1970, the ship broke its moorings and was pushed ashore at the location it remains today. Until 2013, the shipwreck was believed by locals to be the *Sposa*. However, a survey completed by the Shipwreck Preservation Society of Newfoundland and Labrador determined that it was the *Charcot* and, to many people's surprise, the surveyors found two more shipwrecks directly behind the *Charcot* in deeper water: the *Southern Foam* and the *Sukha*.

The *Southern Foam* was a 39.3-metre-long, 7.5-metre-wide steel-hulled ship. Built in 1926 in Middlebrough, England, for whaling at the north and south poles, it was operated by the Southern Whaling & Sealing Company based out of Liverpool, England, where it hunted whales in Antarctica for half the year and the Arctic for the other half. Its career was briefly interrupted during World War II and used by the British Navy as a minesweeper in the North Atlantic. After the war, it returned to whaling on the Labrador coast.

The story of the *Sukha* is similar to that of the *Southern Foam*. Built in 1929 in Middlesbrough, England, this 37.1-metre-long, 7.3-metre-wide ship operated as a whaling ship in the south Atlantic Ocean until it became a minesweeper for the Royal Navy in 1940. In 1948, it was bought by the Polar Whaling Company and operated out of Hawke Harbour, Labrador.

Like the *Charcot*, in 1956 both the *Sukha* and *Southern Foam* were bought by the Hawke Harbour Whaling Company and eventually relocated to a wharf in Conception Harbour. In the same ill-fated 1970 storm that pushed the *Charcot* ashore, the *Sposa* and *Southern Foam* met their fate, sinking to the bottom of the cove.

ABOUT THE AREA

The town of Conception Harbor has embraced the heritage of this site. A small parking lot and picnic area allow visitors to get within several metres of the ship and an informative sign tells how the two ships, resting just several metres from the shore, were found. For those hoping to catch a glimpse of the two sunken wrecks, diving the site or flying a drone over the wrecks during low tides are the best options.

⊕ SS CHARCOT: N 47.444695, W 53.205852

The shipwreck is located in the town of Conception Harbour, just north of Avondale. From the Conception Bay Highway (Route 60), turn north onto Corporal Jamie Murphy Drive. The wreck is located 800 metres on the right.

2. Hamilton Banker

Colliers

Considered an abandoned ship rather than an actual shipwreck, the large fishing vessel *Hamilton Banker* has been left to rust on the shores of Colliers Bay.

The steel ship is 34 metres long and 7.35 metres wide and weighs 360 tons. Built in Norway in 1977, it was refurbished in 1987 for use in Newfoundland. On June 16, 2006, the ship made port in the town of Harbour Grace and the crew unloaded their gear and catch before retiring. When they returned in the morning, the ship had partially sunk and was listing on its starboard side. Emergency crews responded quickly; however, by the time they arrived, little could be done.

Transport Canada and the RCMP discovered the cause of the sinking: a malfunctioning valve. The valve had not shut properly, and as the tide began to rise, the ship got snagged on the wharf and water leaked into the hull. The incident was ruled an accident and the investigation turned over to insurance officials.

On June 20, after divers successfully plugged the hole in the hull, salvage crews pumped out the water and raised the bow out of the water. After many hours of careful manoeuvring, the boat was refloated with the aid of water pumps and cranes. The ship was eventually towed to its current resting place in the community of Colliers.

The ship was beached adjacent to a local fish plant until, in January 2019, a large snowstorm, locally known as Snowmageddon, dislodged the ship and forced it aground across the harbour. The ship remains there to this day.

HAMILTON BANKER: N 47.464794, W 53.207878

North of the community of Conception Harbour on the Conception Bay Highway (Route 60), turn onto Harbour Drive. Drive approximately 2.7 kilometres along the road to view the ship.

3. Brigus Tunnel

Brigus, Conception Bay

Historically the centre of the Newfoundland and Labrador fishery, Brigus was home to prominent merchants, captains, and explorers. The town's small harbour meant that waterfront real estate was in high demand, forcing many of the wealthy citizens to go to extreme lengths to access the sea.

After purchasing a ship to work in the Labrador summer fishery, Captain Abraham Bartlett found himself without a wharf large enough to berth it. Brigus was an ideal location because of its deep and sheltered harbour—but the harbour was overcrowded. Any remaining waterfront was inaccessible and distinguished by steep rocky cliffs. Determined to overcome this, Bartlett hired miner John Hoskins from Cornwall, England, to blast a tunnel through a small rocky ridge to provide access to the opposite side and construct a wharf.

Hoskins, an expert in underground excavation, had been employed at the Tilt Cove Copper Mines on the Baie Verte Peninsula. He began digging the tunnel in the summer of 1860 and finished four months later. To construct the perfectly rectangular tunnel, holes were drilled and filled with gunpowder and blasted in several different sections.

The tunnel measured 2.6 metres high and about 2.4 metres wide, allowing the passage of wheelbarrows, wagons, and even a horse and carriage to aid in the wharf construction on the other side. The tunnel was used until around 1910, when the wharf was no longer required.

Today the tunnel is free to access. Located near the waterfront

behind St. Georges Heritage Church, it is a reminder of the wealth and history that existed in the town.

BRIGUS TUNNEL: N 47.534873, W 53.204878

Driving through the community of Brigus, proceed down Middle Road, following the signs to the tunnel. The tunnel is located beside the road.

4. SS *Kyle*

Harbour Grace, Conception Bay

Although Harbour Grace has a rich aviation history, European settlement, and even pirates, the SS *Kyle* is probably the town's most iconic symbol. The *Kyle* is a remnant of the coastal boat service that once provided supplies and aid to the province's remote communities. It was pushed ashore during a storm in 1967 and left to deteriorate.

HISTORY

The *Kyle*, built in Newcastle-on-Tyne, England, by Swan Hunter & Wigham Richardson Limited for the Reid Newfoundland Company, was constructed for travel along the Newfoundland and Labrador coast, with a strong steel hull to withstand the thick North Atlantic ice floes. On April 17, 1913, the ship began its maiden voyage from England to St. John's.

Named after a town from Robert Reid's home country of Scotland, the *Kyle* joined the Reid Newfoundland Company's Alphabet Fleet and operated as a passenger and cargo vessel. With the help of its six furnace engines and its strengthened hull, the *Kyle* soon gained the reputation as being the strongest and fastest ship in the fleet, capable of reaching speeds of up to 35 kilometres per hour (19 knots).

The *Kyle* was later used as a ferry between Port aux Basques and North Sydney, Nova Scotia, until it was sold to Shaw Steamships Co. Ltd. of Halifax in 1959. Renamed the *Arctic Eagle*, it was transformed into a sealing vessel for use on the Labrador coast. The strengthened hull meant that it could handle

the thick sea ice, icebergs, and long voyages required for the North Atlantic seal hunt.

The ship was re-sold in 1961 for $100,000 to Earle Brothers of Carbonear, who restored its original name, the SS *Kyle*. The *Kyle* participated in the seal hunt for five more years until it was damaged after hitting an iceberg in 1967. The 54-year-old ship sailed back to Harbour Grace for repairs.

On February 4, 1967, the ship broke its moorings from its Harbour Grace dock during a storm and was pushed ashore nearby, in Riverhead. As repairing or salvaging the ship was deemed too expensive, the owners left it where it was. Water flowing into the hull provided the stability to keep it upright. In 1972, the *Kyle* was sold to the provincial government for $4,000 and has remained in the Harbour Grace harbour ever since.

ABOUT THE SHIP

The *Kyle* is one of the last visitable reminders of the Alphabet Fleet. But this piece of heritage is controversial; many deem it an eyesore and say it should be removed. The town of Harbour Grace has recognized the value of the ship, repainting it and creating a heritage garden with a viewing point and historical information.

SS *KYLE*: N 47.670546, W 53.253601

The ship is located at the head of Harbour Grace, along Routes 70 and 75, approximately 40 kilometres north of the Trans-Canada Highway. The shipwreck is clearly visible in the harbour; the viewing point is located near the Kearney Tourist Chalet at the intersection of Water and Harvey Streets.

5. Ridley Hall

Harbour Grace

Ridley Hall exemplifies what happens when our built heritage is neglected. Even though it stands within the Harbour Grace Historical District, its outer walls are all that remain intact.

Constructed in 1834 by prominent fishing/sealing merchant Thomas Ridley, this structure was built from local bluestone and originally possessed a slate gable roof with chimneys on each end. The house, placed on a T-shaped foundation, had a two-storey bay at the front. Ridley Hall's interior once reflected its high-class style, complete with extravagant staircases, expensive furniture, and even a large ballroom at the rear of the building. It's a classic example of the stone structures that were built by the wealthy and a reminder of Harbour Grace's high-class society.

During the mid- to late 19th century, it was the setting for glamorous balls and parties held by the Ridley family. After bankrupting in 1873, Thomas Ridley could no longer maintain the house; it was finally sold after the bank crash in 1894. During the 1930s and 1940s, it was used by the Cable and Wireless Ltd. Company as a cable station. Later, it was once again a private residence, until it was vacated in the 1980s.

The two-storey house was registered as a heritage structure in 1994 but remained empty. In 2003, a fire destroyed its roof and interior, leaving it in its present condition.

 **RIDLEY HALL: N 47.692804, W 53.214550**
Ridley Hall is located at 44 Water Street West.

6. North America's First Civilian Airport

Harbour Grace, Conception Bay

John Alcock and Arthur Brown made the first non-stop transatlantic flight in June 1919. Soon, more and more aircraft were making the 3,000-kilometre trek across the Atlantic. As demand for a departure point somewhere on the east coast of Newfoundland grew, in 1927 Fred Koehler began searching for a place to construct an airfield to cater to those hoping to fly across the Atlantic Ocean. Koehler, a representative of Stinson Aircraft Corporation and Waco

Oil based out of Detroit, Michigan, hoped to encourage more pilots to attempt the flight. During a visit to Harbour Grace, Koehler met with local resident John Oke, who showed him the piece of land where the airstrip is located today.

The idea of an airfield in Harbour Grace garnered widespread support in the area and, on July 25, 1927, a meeting held at the town hall resulted in the creation of the Harbour Grace Airport Trust Company. Seeing the benefits of an airport in Harbour Grace, the Newfoundland government provided a $14,500 grant to cover the cost of constructing the runway and purchasing any necessary machinery.

The construction began shortly afterward and, with the help of the entire community, the airstrip was completed the following month. The 1,219-metre-long, 61-metre-wide gravel runway was considered of exceptional quality for its time, attracting worldwide recognition. On August 26, 1927, Edward F. Schlee and William S. Brock took off from Maine in a small monoplane named the Pride of Detroit and the following day landed at Harbour Grace— making them the first pilots to use the airstrip.

Many famous pilots passed through the Harbour Grace Airport, including aviation pioneer Amelia Earhart, who stopped there on May 20, 1932. After leaving Harbour Grace in a Lockheed Vega, Earhart flew for 14 hours and 56 minutes before landing in Culmore, Ireland. The 34-year-old pilot was the first female to fly solo across the Atlantic.

Earhart is remembered as one of the most inspiring people of the 20th century, as a ground-breaking pilot and for her work to encourage female pilots and gender equality in the industry. In Harbour Grace, a statue and memorial honouring her were placed at the waterfront.

As aircraft technology improved, the distance aircraft could travel without refuelling also improved, eventually making the airfield obsolete and leading to its closure on October 29, 1936. During World War II, the Royal Canadian Navy reopened the airstrip as a base for aircraft to track and intercept German U-boats. It is believed that at least one U-boat was sunk as a result of the aircraft stationed there. After the war ended, the airstrip was again abandoned.

ABOUT THE AREA

In 1977, thanks to the efforts of the Harbour Grace Historical Society, the airfield was restored to operating condition. On November 4, 1999, it was assigned the Official International Identifier CHG2 and listed as a usable and active Canadian Flight Supplement. All that remains are the grassy runway and a few small aircraft hangers.

HARBOUR GRACE AIRSTRIP: N 47.687362, W 53.246913

Beginning in Harbour Grace, follow Lady Lake Road. Pass under Veterans Memorial Highway, continue 600 metres, and turn onto Earhart Strip. The airstrip is located at the end of the short, unpaved road.

7. The Overfalls

Western Bay, Conception Bay North

If you are travelling the Baccalieu Trail (Route 70) along the shores of Conception Bay North, be sure to stop at the Overfalls for a swim, picnic, or a few photos. Overfalls is the name given to a small waterfall in the community of Western Bay that cascades through a narrow valley before flowing into the ocean. After plunging over the edge of the falls, the water pools into a small swimming hole. At one point, the river flows through a rectangular concrete outline. The rectangular feature is a remnant of a past

swimming area that has filled with rocks and debris transported downstream by the river. The waterfall is a welcome pit stop for those travelling up the coast.

⊕ THE OVERFALLS: N 47.886598, W 53.088503

In the community of Western Bay, turn onto Riverhead Road. Drive approximately 150 metres, then turn right onto a gravel road. Park along the road and hike a short distance to its end, where a marked trail guides you down the hill to the falls.

8. Northern Bay Sea Arch

Northern Bay, Conception Bay North

Northern Bay is home to one of the province's few sandy beaches. Located at the head of the bay, near Northern Bay Brook, the beach is relatively well known and well visited each summer. But what is often missed by visitors is a large sea arch overlooking the beach, on the north side of the bay. The sea arch is located on a rocky beach that lies underneath the arch, allowing visitors to walk through the arch.

◎ **NORTHERN BAY SEA ARCH:** N 47.941277, W 53.072032

The nearest access is in the community of Northern Bay along Route 70. By parking near the intersection of Oliver's Road and Route 70, it is possible to hike between house properties to the cliffside. A steep descent to the sheltered beach below brings you to the sea arch. Most of the land is privately owned, so do not trespass or disturb residents.

9. Mouse Hole Arch

Burnt Point, Conception Bay North

Hidden among the coastal cliffs of Conception Bay North is Mouse Hole Arch, a sea arch carved into the rocky peninsula protruding into the bay. When you are driving north on the Conception Bay Highway, it is easy to miss the arch unless you look in the rearview mirror at the right time. In the summer, be sure to also check the rugged coastline for icebergs.

⊕ **MOUSE HOLE ARCH:** N 47.961735, W 53.032905

The best viewing point for the arch is via a short accessible walk to the cliffside, starting at the end of Main Street (N 47.958769, W 53.033213) in the community of Burnt Point. Another viewing location is along Route 70, approximately 500 metres past the turnoff to Main Street and the Sea Arch Efficiency Units.

10. New Harbour Trout Farm Project
New Harbour/Hopeall, Trinity Bay

Between the communities of Hopeall and New Harbour in Trinity Bay are the remains of a rather unusual project. In order to test the viability of aquaculture in the province, in the 1970s a trout farm was constructed there. This series of water canals, dams, and buildings were left to deteriorate. While it is clear that the project did not succeed as expected, it was once hoped it would bring a new industry, and new life, to nearby towns and communities.

HISTORY

In 1974, the idea to build a rainbow trout farm near the community of New Harbour was proposed by the Greens Harbour Development Committee. The project, officially titled the Upper Trinity South Regional Development Association Rainbow Trout Fish Farm Pilot Project, consisted of three one-year stages; it would be tested at each stage and, if successful, expand to the next. The first phase was approved and in 1975 construction began on what would become the province's first commercial fish farm, laying the foundations for future pisciculture.

While the fish hatchery originally planned to bring in fish from Ontario, the federal government prohibited transporting fish between provinces to reduce the potential for disease transmission. This delayed the project until the federal Fisheries and Marine Services agreed to supply a breeder within Newfoundland.

The facility operated by allowing water to flow through a gravity-fed pipeline that supplied the hatchery from nearby Island Pond. The water entered the main building of the complex and distributed into two indoor and three outdoor pools, or raceways. These 12-metre-long, 2.5-metre-wide concrete raceways provided a habitat for the fingerlings until they grew large enough to be introduced into the next raceway. Once the fish had grown, they were moved to a grow-out facility of net cages in Greens Harbour.

While in operation, the hatchery provided many jobs to nearby communities. But its days were numbered: contaminants leaking from an old landfill located upstream were detected, likely the reason the facility closed in the late 1990s.

The trout hatchery is an intriguing place. Many of the buildings have fallen down, but the raceways and water channels continue to move water throughout the complex. The source of this water is a strange feature: a vertical column of water pouring out from the ground. The source: the broken end of a 400-metre-long underground water pipeline that transported water from Island Pond to the hatchery. After the water runs through the complex, it is discharged into a channelized section of Hopeall River. A dam redirects water from the main river into the channel.

In 2012, a proposal to use some of the remaining trout hatchery infrastructure was made to the provincial government, but the project was never implemented.

 **HATCHERY:** N 47.590812, W 53.502024

There are two trails to the hatchery. The first trailhead (N 47.581954, W 53.515339) is located along Route 73, approximately 150 metres east of the intersection with Route 80. From here, travel 1.5 kilometres along the gravel road. Shortly after crossing Hopeall River, turn left onto a small path and continue for another 200 metres.

The second trailhead (N 47.600631, W 53.500523) is along Route 80, approximately 2.4 kilometres north of the intersection with Route 73. From here, travel approximately 1.3 kilometres along the gravel road before turning right onto a small path and continuing for another 200 metres.

11. Hopeall Falls

New Harbour/Hopeall, Trinity Bay

Rushing out of Island Pond, Hopeall River flows under the old Route 80 highway bridge and descends into a deep, narrow gorge, producing Hopeall Falls. The spectacular waterfall can be viewed up close, thanks to several trails that wind through the forest and small gorge. The falls were located much closer to the original highway than they are to the current one and, because of this, a small campground was built near the top of the falls. As you walk along the rim of the gorge and along the hiking trails required to get to the falls, the camping sites are still clearly visible.

For those willing to brave the murky water beneath the falls, this location is also suitable for swimming.

HOPEALL FALLS: N 47.589133, W 53.500748

Located on Route 80, approximately 1.4 kilometres north of the turnoff to Route 73, a parking lot and sign mark the trailhead (N 47.592487, W 53.505978). From there, a 1-kilometre-long hike brings you to the falls.

The waterfall is also accessible by way of the old highway (now a gravel road) with entrances along Route 80 (N 47.600631, W 53.500523) and Route 73 (N 47.581954, W 53.515339). From the trailhead located south of the Hopeall River Bridge, a short, easy walk leads to the falls.

12. Chance Cove Coastal Trail

Chance Cove, Trinity Bay

The seaside town of Chance Cove, located at the bottom of Trinity Bay, at the furthest reach of Route 16, is home to sea arches, sandy beaches, and steep coastal cliffs. But perhaps nothing exemplifies the beauty of southern Trinity Bay better than the Chance Cove Coastal Trail. This 4-kilometre-long trail passes by the sandy Chance Cove Beach, rounds Green Head, and leads to a lookout overlooking Chance Cove Island, Island Cove Beach, Patrick's Cove, and Big Cove.

Patrick's Cove features a large beach that curves around the cove before joining an enormous sea stack that has separated from the cliffside. The dark rocks that contrast with the green grass and tree-covered hills formed over 600 million years ago.

⊕ **CHANCE COVE COASTAL TRAIL:** N 47.666711, W 53.812858

The trailhead for the Chance Cove Coastal Trail is in the town of Chance Cove, approximately 5.6 kilometres from the Trans-Canada Highway. The trailhead and parking are located along Route 16.

13. Collier Point Barite Mine
Norman's Cove-Long Cove, Trinity Bay

A barren hillside, water-filled trenches, and several abandoned structures are all that remain of the Collier Point Barite Mine. Since barite was discovered in the area in the early 20th century, it has been the subject of exploratory surveys and viability studies, but only two successful small-scale mining attempts.

The mine was first operated between 1902 and 1904 by the Collier Cove Barite Company, owned by Robert Rendell. The company extracted 5,075 tons of barite from an open pit and a 40-metre-deep vertical shaft located on top of the hill. The barite was sold to North American paint companies. After 1904, operations ceased, and it was many years before the mine was active again. In 1951, Toronto-based mining investors took samples to determine the viability of using the mine's remaining barite for the production of drilling mud. While the barite was of high grade, the amount believed to be found at Collier Point was too little for a viable mining operation.

This did not stop J. Tyler Mining Ltd. In 1980, the company built a road to the deposit and extracted approximately 9,000 tons of ore from a newly dug open pit atop the hill. The company sold the ore for use in the processing of drilling mud. Since then, further exploration surveys have been completed, but the mine remains dormant.

The hilltop is reached by a 3-kilometre-long hike up a dirt path. Abandoned buildings and rusted equipment are littered through the woods and at the top of the hill the open-pit mine is difficult to miss. And while the area's mining past is well concealed, panoramic views of Norman's Cove and Thornlea make the hike worthwhile.

◎ **BARITE MINE:** N 47.586957 W 53.686624

The trailhead (N 47.562046, W 53.694276) is located approximately 1 kilometre west of the town of Norman's Cove-Long Cove along Route 201. From here, hike 3 kilometres along the gravel road to the mine. The site has undergone numerous ownership changes and mineral prospecting expeditions, so proceed with caution.

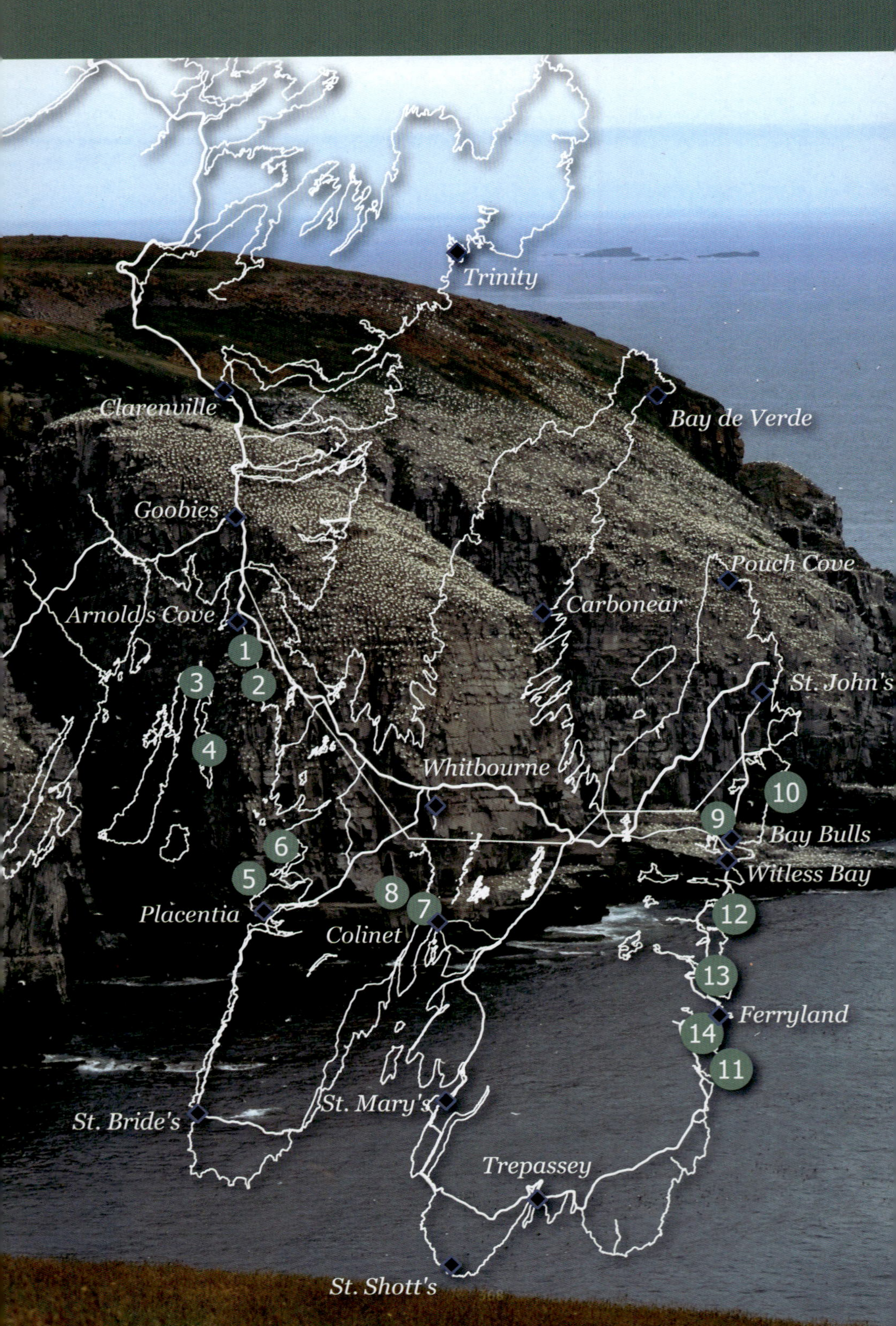

Trinity
Clarenville
Bay de Verde
Goobies
Pouch Cove
Carbonear
Arnolds Cove
1
3
2
St. John's
4
Whitbourne
10
9
Bay Bulls
6
Witless Bay
5
8
7
12
Placentia
Colinet
13
Ferryland
14
11
St. Mary's
St. Bride's
Trepassey
St. Shott's

Placentia Bay & the Southern Avalon Peninsula

Placentia Bay and the southern Avalon Peninsula contain a diverse range of landscapes. Most of Placentia Bay, one of the largest bays in the province, remains remote. On the east side of the bay is the town of Placentia, first established by France to assert its claim to the land. South along the coastline, St. Mary's Ecological Reserve is a natural wonder, located on the edge of a cliff where thousands of sea birds live, eat, and breed each year. In the middle of the Avalon Peninsula, forest, rolling hills, and rivers surround St. Mary's Bay. Travel south along the Irish Loop to see traditional fishing communities, as well as vast stretches of barren, boggy landscape. Travel to communities such as Ferryland to see stone churches, fishing stages, and seaside houses backdropped by the ocean and fog that hovers just offshore.

The area contains some of the first European settlements on the island. Although the French established Plaisance (later anglicized to Placentia), on the opposite side of the peninsula the English established the Colony of Avalon, now known as Ferryland. Conflicts between the two countries dictated how settlements evolved across the region. Eventually the English dominated. Bustling merchant and fishing communities were established to serve those participating in the Grand Banks fishery, the seal hunt, and the whaling industry. Many of Placentia Bay's islands were, for a time, dotted with communities. During the resettlement programs of the late 20th century, almost every community not located near a major transportation network was resettled.

In 1941, the establishment of one of the province's largest naval bases in Argentia vastly changed the area, helping the town of Placentia become the small service centre it is today. And while the fishing industry continues to be a factor in the region, its decline has led to many former residents moving to larger centres such as St. John's.

Many places hidden among the nooks and crannies of Placentia Bay remain accessible only to those with the ability to travel the dangerous bay by boat. As for the rest of the Avalon Peninsula, the Trans-Canada Highway is the easiest east-to-west route. Along the north shore of Placentia Bay, small highways connect some of the remaining coastal communities; from Whitbourne, take Route 100 to Placentia, and Route 81 to Colinet and Mt. Carmel-Mitchells Brook-St. Catherine's in St. Mary's Bay. These towns are also accessible via Salmonier Line (Route 90), which encircles the east side of the Avalon, forming the Irish Loop, a popular driving route. On the west side of the peninsula, Route 100 travels through Placentia and loops around Point Lance and Cape St. Mary's.

1. La Manche Lead Mine

La Manche, Placentia Bay

Located on the north side of Placentia Bay is the La Manche lead mine, discovered in 1855 by the Telegraph Land Company while surveying a route to place a transatlantic cable which was to enter Trinity Bay and cross into Placentia Bay.

The first mine was operated by Ripley and Company. The Placentia Lead Mine Company took control of the mine in 1860 and operated it until its first closure in 1873, extracting about 3,175 tonnes of galena, a highly concentrated lead mineral. The mine was reopened periodically over the next 50 years, but low ore content, excavation difficulties, and flooding in the mine shafts prevented each endeavour from being profitable.

In 1928, the mine was transferred to the Newfoundland Mining Corporation. In 1929, the Corporation sank a 120-metre-deep shaft into the ore layer with multiple horizontal layers of "drifts." Once again, the mine did not remain in production for long; it closed due to financial difficulties. An estimated 196,200 tonnes of ore remained to be mined.

In 1946, the Buchans Mining Company acquired a 99-year lease for the property. After extensive research and prospecting, the mine was found to not be economically viable and reverted to Crown land in 1972.

In the late 1970s, an immense geochemical, soil, and geologic investigation took place in the area and several trenches were dug down to the bedrock. The investigation did not discover any new deposits, and the site was once again abandoned.

ABOUT THE AREA

The mine lies in a small gully on the shore of Placentia Bay. As the river enters the site, it flows over a small concrete dam and into a small underground opening left over from the mining operation. If you follow the narrow gully toward the shore, large tailings piles of unused ore and partly buried equipment are visible. As you approach the beach along the shore, the river re-emerges and flows through a tall, narrow gorge and onto the beach. The river's entrance and exit mark the remains of the mine shafts. Signs throughout the area warn of open holes; exercise caution when exploring.

LA MANCHE LEAD MINE: N 47.687274, W 53.940488

Approximately 39 kilometres east of Whitbourne on the Trans-Canada Highway, turn onto Main Road toward Little Harbour East. Travel for 2 kilometres, turning onto a gravel road (N 47.665935, W 53.907467). Continue for approximately 5 kilometres and turn left onto a small ATV trail. Another 1.5 kilometres brings you to the mine (toward the south) and the abandoned community of La Manche (to the north).

2. La Manche Community

Placentia Bay

A grassy hillside is all that remains of the small fishing community of La Manche (not to be confused with the provincial park and resettled community north of Ferryland). The first census records 20 residents in 1833, but the discovery of galena (a form of lead) nearby instigated a mining boom, resulting in a population of 142 by 1874.

While the protected harbour was an ideal location for fishers to anchor their ships, the inshore fishery was overshadowed by mining. The community thrived for many years but the mining venture did not last long, and the population dwindled through the late 1800s. The fishery supported those who decided to stay, until the resettlement programs of the mid-20th century. The last census of the area, completed in 1966, indicated one resident.

Today La Manche is a barren hillscape but offers views of Placentia Bay and a coast scattered with sea caves, sea arches, and other intriguing rock formations, and is a popular destination for ATV and snowmobile enthusiasts.

LA MANCHE: N 47.691466, W 53.940232

Approximately 39 kilometres east of Whitbourne on the Trans-Canada Highway, turn onto Main Road toward Little Harbour East. Travel for 2 kilometres, turning onto a gravel road (N 47.665935, W 53.907467). Continue 5 kilometres and turn left onto a small ATV trail. 1.5 kilometres brings you to the mine (to the south) and the abandoned community of La Manche (to the north).

3. Spencer's Cove

Long Island, Placentia Bay

Located on Placentia Bay's second largest island, the resettled community of Spencer's Cove was once a bustling fishing community. Archeologic evidence suggests that the sheltered cove was first used by the Dorset Paleo-Eskimos as a seasonal hunting camp. By the mid-19th century inshore fishers had established a community. The first census, in 1857, showed 87 residents.

Toward the end of the century, Spencer's Cove became a major hub for lobster trading. In the early 20th century, Alberto Wareham established a small mercantile business there. Alberto Wareham and Sons soon became one of the main exporters of lobster and suppliers of the inshore fishery in the bay. In the early 1960s, a fire destroyed Wareham's Spencer's Cove premises and Wareham moved his business to nearby Arnold's Cove. This eventually resulted in the complete resettlement of Spencer's Cove by 1966.

The sheltered, grass-lined cove is a quiet oasis, protected from the harsh conditions typically experienced in Placentia Bay. Concrete pathways, house foundations, and remains of the Wareham premises lie along the beachfront. Cabins and summer homes are owned by former residents or people with family ties to the community.

SPENCER'S COVE: N 47.665578, W 54.085080

A boat is required to reach Spencer's Cove, which is located approximately 15 kilometres southwest of Arnold's Cove. Placentia Bay is often a dangerous bay to navigate, and proper knowledge of both the area and the ocean is essential.

4. *Fumi Maru No. 15* Shipwreck
Harbour Buffet, Placentia Bay

Rusting on the coast of Long Island, Placentia Bay, is the wreck of the *Fumi Maru No. 15*. The ship was once used to hunt whales along Newfoundland's coast; after the industry was banned, the ship was no longer needed. It was then tied to a wharf in the now-resettled community of Harbour Buffet until a storm caused it to break its moorings and become lodged on the rocky shoreline nearby.

The ship's story begins in December 1966. The Japanese-Canadian Atlantic Whaling Company was formed between the Taiyo Fishing Company and Canadian Fishery Products. In its first year of operation, the company contracted the whaler *Fumi Maru No. 15* to hunt fin whales in the North Atlantic. It had a crew of 14, seven of whom were Newfoundlanders, and operated out of the Williamsport Whaling Station on the Northern Peninsula. In its first season, in 1967, its catch of 262 fin whales exceeded expectations.

The ship, built in south Japan in 1952, was 50 metres long, with a gross tonnage of 427 tonnes. Prior to its career in Newfoundland, it operated out of the South Pacific Ocean, where it made regular fishing and whaling trips to Antarctica.

The ship continued whaling until 1972, when the whaling industry in Canada was closed. After this, it was brought to Argentia and tied up to a wharf to await a decision on its future. The wharf was soon required for other uses and the ship was towed across Placentia Bay to the recently resettled community of Harbour Buffet. Shortly after this, a storm caused the ship to break from its moorings and pushed it aground; it remains there today.

FUMI MARU NO. 15: N 47.523736, W 54.083529

The ship lies aground in Harbour Buffet on Long Island in Placentia Bay. A boat is required to reach the harbour, which is located approximately 13 kilometres west of the community of Fair Haven.

5. Argentia Naval Air Base & Fort McAndrew

Argentia, Placentia Bay

One of the largest military bases in the province during World War II and the Cold War was the Argentia Naval Air Base and Fort McAndrew. The base, constructed on a large, flat peninsula that extends out into Placentia Bay near the town of Placentia, consisted of a large airfield, dockyard, and submarine base, as well as an adjacent army base named Fort McAndrew. At its peak, 20,000 American servicemen were stationed at Argentia.

The remains of this vast military complex are visible today. While most of the original structures have been torn down, concrete bunkers and coastal defence batteries lie throughout the hills surrounding the harbour and the airfield runways are still driveable.

HISTORY

Before 1940, Argentia was a small fishing community whose population did not exceed 500 people. Aside from fishing, the only other user of the small but deep ice-free harbour was the Newfoundland Railway Company, who established a supply dock there in the early 20th century.

But as World War II raged on, new defence bases and convoy protection bases were imperative. In 1940, the signing of the Destroyers for Bases Agreement between the US and Britain allotted 3,392 acres of land on a large peninsula in Placentia Bay to the United States Navy to construct a naval air station.

Immediately following the agreement, the US Department of Defense began surveying and preparing for the base. On

October 13, 1940, the first US Corps of Engineers and civilian hydrographers and surveyors arrived at Argentia aboard the USS *Bowditch*. The next ship to arrive was the USS *Richard Peck*, which entered the harbour on January 18, carrying 1,500 construction workers and engineers. The *Richard Peck* remained tied up at the dock in Argentia, serving as temporary barracks for workers until proper living quarters could be built.

To make way for the base, approximately 750 people in the communities of Argentia and Marquise were relocated to the nearby town of Placentia. Although many were upset at the news, the residents generally co-operated because of the high number of jobs the base was expected to create.

Construction crews worked quickly to build the $53 million base, making it one of the most expensive overseas American

military installations of World War II. Once completed, the airfield contained three runways, measuring roughly 1,680 metres, 1,620 metres, and 2,130 metres, a 600-metre wharf, a floating drydock, hangars, living quarters, and storage space for 56 million litres of gasoline, oil, and jet fuel. A branch line of the Newfoundland Railway was constructed to connect the base to the national railway network. When the base was completed, approximately 240,000 cubic metres of peat, gravel, and rock had been excavated, moved, and compacted to construct the airfield.

On July 15, 1941, Naval Operating Base Argentia was officially commissioned and on August 28, Naval Air Station Argentia was officially commissioned. Operations began immediately. Navy ships rallied at Argentia before sailing across the Atlantic, while protecting supply and passenger ships from enemy U-boats.

Coastal patrol and anti-submarine aircraft began patrolling the coast for German U-boat activity.

In March 1942, the US Army established a base adjacent to the peninsula containing the naval base. The base, named Fort McAndrew, provided security to the naval base using a series of anti-aircraft and coastal defence batteries. Fort McAndrew also served as a base for an infantry company, a coastal artillery group, and an anti-motor torpedo battalion.

In the spring of 1943, a 7,000-ton floating drydock was installed at Argentia to repair Navy ships. By this time, thousands of US Navy, Marine, and Army troops had passed through Argentia on their way to Europe and, by the end of the war, this grew to over 10,000. When the war ended, the number of personnel working at Argentia quickly decreased and it appeared that the US would no longer require the base's operations.

However, a potentially more devastating war was just beginning. As tensions increased between the Soviet Union and the US, the Argentia base underwent many upgrades. In 1946,

Fort McAndrew was transferred to the US Army Air Force and in 1948 renamed McAndrew Air Force Base. At this time, 7,000 naval and marine troops were stationed at Argentia.

Once again Argentia's strategic location made it the centre of operations for patrolling the North Atlantic. Soviet nuclear submarines were the most imminent threat to the US, and because of this, many advanced radar and surveillance systems were installed at Argentia. One such system, an advanced, top-secret network known as SOSUS (Sound Surveillance System), was designed to detect Soviet submarines and Navy vessels that attempted to cross the Atlantic Ocean.

The American presence at Argentia again increased in 1950 as the Korean War began. Several years later, when this war ended, the base was slowly phased out. McAndrew Air Force Base was decommissioned in 1955 and its facilities turned over to the US Navy. Most of the air force personnel were transferred to other bases in the province, such as the Harmon Air Force Base in Stephenville.

The base's main task then became offering support to the 64th Air Division and North American Aerospace Defense Command (NORAD), both operating early warning radar systems in the province. Argentia now hosted east coast fighter jet squadrons, which intercepted any unidentified or enemy aircraft.

Throughout the 1950s and 1960s, Argentia continued to perform an important role in monitoring the Soviet Union and as a refuelling location for naval ships and aircraft travelling across the Atlantic. But as radar systems and aircraft ranges improved, Argentia slowly became obsolete. In 1973, Naval Air Station Argentia was almost entirely decommissioned. Most of the land comprising the base was transferred to the Canadian government in 1975 and later to the Newfoundland government.

The US Navy continued to operate several buildings in the area until officially decommissioning Naval Air Station Argentia in 1994. During the decommissioning period, all buildings were transferred to the federal government. It was reported that many buildings containing sensitive and "secret" equipment were demolished or buried by the US before completing the transfer.

ABOUT THE AREA

The area is an example of adaptive reuse. The paved airfield is now used partially as an industrial area and storage lot. Parts of the original wharf are used by the inter-provincial ferry system operated by Marine Atlantic and as a refuelling/resupply station for the Canadian Coast Guard. In 2017, Husky Energy announced that it would build a fixed wellhead platform on the northeast side of the old airfield. Except for Placentia Bay's harsh weather, the large, flat area of land and its deepwater bay made this a perfect location to construct the dry dock required by the company.

 **SOUTHERN LOOKOUT BATTERIES:** N 47.261709, W 53.991282

Overlooking the south side of Fort McAndrew, in the most southern extremity of the base, is a series of lookout batteries known as Pillboxes, due to their shape. These concrete structures are dug into the hillside overlooking southern Placentia Bay. That they are more exposed than most batteries in the province provides a unique way to see these normally buried structures.

BUNKER HILL: N 47.274994, W 53.977003

In the hills above Fort McAndrew are several ammunition bunkers. Similar to bunkers in other military bases across Newfoundland, these concrete structures, or "igloos," were built with thick, reinforced steel and covered in vegetation as camouflage to aircraft flying overhead. Each bunker contained just one large room with a blast-proof door. Today most of these remain in relatively good shape and some are still used to store equipment and materials.

UNDERGROUND COMMAND AND CONTROL BUNKER: N 47.276127, W 53.986584

Located near the intersection of Marquis Avenue and Charter Avenue in the former Fort McAndrew Base is one of the largest underground structures built at Argentia. As with many secret bunkers, information about it is scarce. Local reports suggest that

this enormous two-storey bunker was used as both an emergency hospital and a Command and Control (CNC) centre for the two coastal defence batteries nearby. The bunker is about 50 metres long and extends into the hill approximately 20 metres.

The CNC bunker is a must-see for anyone interested in New-foundland and Labrador's military history. And while the bunker is accessible, poor air quality, risk of asbestos/mould, and deteriorating structural conditions make it too dangerous to enter.

COASTAL DEFENCE BATTERIES 281 AND 282

Coastal Defence Batteries 281 and 282 were constructed of reinforced concrete and covered in gravel and soil as camouflage. They were built in Fort McAndrew to protect the Argentia Naval Air Station from German U-boat attacks.

The batteries were "200 series" coastal defence batteries. Each contained a main underground operation and ammunition storage, with two 150-millimetre guns mounted on either side. Each battery had its own power generation and water systems. The two 150-millimetre M1905A2 rapid-fire guns were mounted on M1 Shielded Barbette Carriages. The barrel length of the guns was 7.7 metres and each could fire a 105-pound armor-piercing projectile up to 24 kilometres. Each gun was capable of firing five of these every minute.

 **BATTERY 282:** N 47.273862, W 53.989318

Located on top of a small hill overlooking the airfield, Battery 282 is one of the best-preserved coastal defence batteries on the island. In 2005, it was designated a registered heritage structure with the Heritage Foundation of Newfoundland and Labrador.

 **BATTERY 281:** N 47.290212, W 53.979389

Battery 281 is not designated a heritage site. In 1994, the guns, carriages, and shields were removed and put on display at Fort Columbia in Washington state. The concrete platforms that once supported the guns are still visible as well as the underground support structure are visible.

ARGENTIA: N 47.287832, W 53.994160

Argentia is located north of the town of Placentia and the easiest way to find it is to follow the signs for the Marine Atlantic Terminal. This is located at the end of Route 100, approximately 43 kilometres south of the town of Whitbourne and the Trans-Canada Highway. Gravel and paved roads allow explorers to drive through the old base.

6. Isaac Head Battery

Fox Harbour, Placentia Bay

During the construction of the Argentia Naval Base, a military lookout battery was established across Placentia Sound on Isaac Point. The battery was built at the end of a small finger of land protruding into the bay and located about halfway up one of the two distinctive, pointed hills known as Isaac Head. Under the control and supervision of Fort McAndrew nearby, the battery consisted of three concrete bunkers embedded into the grassy hillside. Built in 1940 and officially named Battery 955, it was equipped with a 76-millimetre gun that could protect the airfield from aircraft or enemy U-boats as well as multiple 90-millimetre anti-aircraft guns and several searchlights.

Access to the site was primarily by boat, which landed at a nearby cove that also contained several barracks to support those working there. From the cove a road was carved into the side of the hill and up the headland to the site. The only way to get to the battery today is by hiking from nearby Fox Harbour or by boat.

ISAAC HEAD BATTERY: N 47.322603, W 53.950417

No trail to the site exists. The nearest access is from nearby Fox Harbour. Leaving from the end of Green Road in Fox Harbour (N 47.322158, W 53.919772), follow the beach around the harbour and adjacent cove. After about 3 kilometres, the beach ends; hike over the forested Isaac Head to arrive in a small cove and the start of the grassy road leading to the battery.

7. Rocky River Waterfall & Bridge

Colinet, St. Mary's Bay

Rocky River winds through the flat interior of the Avalon Peninsula. For the most part, the wide, gently flowing river is a backcountry waterway suitable for canoers, kayakers, and fishers. But as the river approaches St. Mary's Bay, it abruptly plunges over a 3-metre-high waterfall and then immediately over an 8-metre-high waterfall. Below the waterfalls, the river widens out as it enters an estuary-like river, much deeper than above the falls. The picturesque valley complements the cascades of the waterfall.

Spanning the falls are the old and new Old Placentia Highway bridges. The newer bridge located farther upstream was constructed in 1990 to replace its aging predecessor. But the design of the new bridge is hardly worth noticing, next to the architectural beauty of its neighbour. The older bridge was designed by T.A. Hall and his assistant W.J. Robinson and constructed between May and October 1922. It resembles the bridge in nearby Cataracts Provincial Park and is used as a pedestrian bridge. It provides a vantage point from

above the falls that is away from the nearby busy road.

The river's outflow into the ocean meant that it had the potential to become a successful salmon river, if not for the waterfall near its mouth. In 1987, an elaborate fish ladder was built to scale the falls, and salmon were introduced upstream. This attempt to populate the river was successful, and nearly 20 years later, it was opened as the island's newest salmon river. The fish ladder is visible on the west side of the river.

The use of the old bridge as a lookout and an accessible walking trail that lets viewers look back on the falls makes this site accessible to all. For those looking for another view of the falls, it is possible to paddle up the river and witness it from below. Leave from the town of Colinet.

ROCKY RIVER BRIDGE: N 47.225709, W 53.567499

Rocky River is approximately 1.2 kilometres west of Colinet on the Old Placentia Highway (Route 91). Parking is available across the bridge.

8. Cataracts Provincial Park

Colinet, St. Mary's Bay

West of the town of Colinet on the unpaved Route 91, this small provincial park is located where the Cataracts River and another smaller unnamed brook cascade down into a deep narrow gorge. Spanning the gorge is the Ellis Memorial Bridge, built in 1926, named for William J. Ellis, who led the construction of the bridge but passed away before it was completed.

A short boardwalk encircles the gorge, providing easy access and views of the gorge, waterfall, and bridge. Although it is designated a provincial park, the gorge itself is not well marked and can be easily missed. Be sure to add a stop at this location to any trip to the St. Mary's Ecological Reserve or drive along the Irish Loop.

 **CATARACTS PROVINCIAL PARK:** N 47.242081, W 53.631703

The bridge and gorge are located immediately off Route 90, approximately 8 kilometres west of Colinet. While the unpaved road to the area is a well-maintained provincial highway, it can become muddy and rough during heavy rain events or the spring of the year.

9.   Bay Bulls Hydroelectric Facility
Bay Bulls

The town of Bay Bulls, south of St. John's, has a long rich history as a fishing outport. But its most notable industry boom came during World War II, when its harbour was chosen as the location for a marine repair dockyard for military and supply ships. Built between 1942 and 1944 by the Royal Canadian Navy, the facility operated for approximately one year before the end of the war made the yard obsolete.

During dockyard construction, the harbour was transformed by new buildings, warehouses, repair yards, and a hydroelectric dam. Built on the Bay Bulls River, the dam diverted water through a pipeline that relatively followed Lower Path before plunging over the hillside and into a small electric generation plant close to the town. The plant's location at the bottom of a steep cliff on an inaccessible side of the river makes it difficult to access.

At the base of the mountain, the concrete shell of the hydro plant, along with several pieces of equipment, is still visible along the edge of the river. Along Lower Path Road is the near-vertical penstock that delivered the water to the plant. Following Lower Path Road farther are the trailhead to a popular swimming hole and the facilities dam.

While the shipyard laid the foundations for the marine terminal established in the town today, little remains of the World War II marine base. The hydroelectric building is one of the last reminders of the short-lived boom that happened in the town during World War II.

HYDROELECTRIC FACILITY: N 47.324444, W 52.818859

The building is difficult to access. Leave from the Bay Bulls Regional Lifestyle Centre on Cemetery Lane and hike through the forest for approximately 40 metres to the river. The building is located approximately 200 metres upstream on the opposite side of the river.

10. The Spout

Spout Path, East Coast Trail

A highlight of the East Coast Trail, the Spout cannot be classified as an unknown place, but its isolated location certainly qualifies it as hidden. Located along the trail between Petty Harbour and Bay Bulls, the Spout is a geomorphic feature officially called a blowhole or marine geyser. Other blowholes exist on the island but they are rare and typically smaller than the Spout. A blowhole is formed when waves erode the underside of rocks either partly or completely under water. As ocean waves and swells enter the hole, they push a column of air and water straight up. The result is a volcanic-like explosion of water. The blowhole south of Petty Harbour, known as the Spout, is a popular destination for backpackers and longer-distance hikers. The feature is best seen when waves and swells are attacking from the east.

THE SPOUT: N 47.366050, W 52.726375

The most popular way to travel to the Spout is to hike the East Coast Trail. The trailheads are located in Petty Harbour (N 47.463217, W 52.704290) and Bay Bulls (N 47.311969, W 52.784939). Hike for approximately 13.5 kilometres (from Petty Harbour) and 12.7 kilometres (from Bay Bulls) to the Spout.

A shorter, yet less scenic route is also possible from Shoal Cove Road (N 47.436085, W 52.759048) in Kilbride, St. John's. Park at the end of the road, hike along the ATV trail for approximately 6.2 kilometres to the ocean, and follow the East Coast Trail south for 4.5 kilometres.

11. SS *Ilex*

Kingman's Cove, Fermeuse

Resting on its side on the south side of Fermeuse harbour is the shipwreck of the SS *Ilex*. The ship came to rest after a fire broke out in its hull in 1948. Although everyone on board made it off safely, the ship was beyond repair, and purposely run aground. Today, the *Ilex* is in two pieces, broken apart by the unforgiving sea. It can be seen from a viewing point across the harbour, but it is best experienced close up via a short hike down the south side beach. The *Ilex* is a must-visit location for those travelling the Irish Loop.

HISTORY

On October 27, 1948, the SS *Ilex* left St. John's en route to Kingston, Jamaica, with a shipment of salt fish. Shortly after the ship's departure, an approaching storm forced the captain to take shelter in Fermeuse harbour. The crew secured the ship and tied up to a dock in Kingman's Cove.

However, shortly after docking, a fire, caused by the ignition of fuel in the ship's oil-fired boiler room, broke out. According to the *Western Star*, chief engineer Arch Sutherland was nearly killed by the initial backdraft explosion. Luckily, the entire crew escaped by lifeboat just before the ship was fully engulfed by flames.

The ship reportedly smouldered for several days and, even though most of the cargo was saved, the unsalvageable ship was run aground in a nearby cove.

ABOUT THE AREA

A short hike up the beach in Fermeuse allows you to get close to the remains of the 70-year-old ship. Even though it is relatively in good condition, it has not been turned into a tourist attraction like so many others around the province (e.g., SS *Charcot* or SS *Kyle*).

The most accessible place to view the ship is across the harbour on the road to Port Kirwan. For those wishing to venture

closer, a short hike along the rocky beach in Kingman's Cove brings you alongside the remains.

⊕ *SS ILEX*: N 46.965147, W 52.923691

Travel along Route 10 through the town of Fermeuse, turn onto King Cove Road. Travel about 2.5 kilometres and park along the side of the road. No trail exists to the site; a short hike over the hillside and east along the beach is required to get to the wreck.

To see the shipwreck from your car, a viewing point (N 46.970206, W 52.920789) is located on the north side of Fermeuse harbour on Port Kirwan Road.

12. La Manche

La Manche Provincial Park

Along the Irish Loop (Route 10) between Tors Cove and Cape Broyle is La Manche Provincial Park. Opened in August 1966, La Manche Provincial Park offers hiking, whale watching, camping, and swimming. The park was so named after a small resettled fishing community that was located on the rocky coastline. The name La Manche is derived from the French word for sleeve, which describes the narrow, steep-sided cove in which the community was located. In the 17th century, the French sailors who named the cove likely used it to hide from English ships during the French raids on the English settlements of Ferryland and St. John's.

The community was first settled around 1840 by George Melvin, who was followed by relatives. According to the 1845 census, seven people lived in the cove. The community continued to grow and, in 1919, a small school was built for children in the lower grades. Children in the higher grades were expected to walk 8 kilometres to school in Tors Cove. At its peak in 1949, the community contained 13 houses, with 54 residents, a Roman Catholic church, stores, and fishing flakes built along the cliffs and shoreline.

After 1949, residents began relocating to larger towns. By 1961, only 25 residents remained. With a diminishing population and the difficulty of maintaining road access, the people of La Manche were increasingly pressured to relocate.

On January 25, 1966, a powerful winter storm hit the east coast of the island. A combination of high tides and waves washed many boats, flakes, stores, and the original suspension

bridge connecting both sides of La Manche harbour out to sea. The destruction of the village was enough to cause the remaining residents to relocate.

Today, several building foundations, stairs, and rock walls are all that remain of this once bustling fishing community. The site is located on the East Coast Trail and, in 1999, a suspension bridge was built over the harbour by the East Coast Trail Association.

LA MANCHE VILLAGE: N 47.166524, W 52.866958

Travel south on Route 10 (the Irish Loop), turn left onto La Manche Road, located 1.6 kilometres south of the entrance to La Manche Provincial Park. Travel approximately 1.8 kilometres to the end of the gravel road to the trailhead (N 47.162612, W 52.880435). A 1.4-kilometre-long trail brings you to the abandoned community and suspension bridge.

13. Spout River Falls
Aquaforte

Spout River waterfall can be seen only from the waters of Aquaforte Harbour or from a drone. The river plunges over the cliff face directly into the ocean, creating a small rocky beach at its base and adding to the scenery of the bay. The inaccessible waterfall is a reminder of the many hidden wonders along the Newfoundland coast and, while it is difficult to see, this exclusivity may just add to its charm.

SPOUT RIVER FALLS: N 47.010310, W 52.925869

Although it is possible to see the falls by following Spout River to its terminus, no trail exists to the falls. The best way to see the falls is by boating or sea kayaking along the north shore of Aquaforte harbour approximately 2.5 kilometres east of the town of Aquaforte.

14. Berry Head Sea Arch

Spurwink Island Path, East Coast Trail

This sea arch is located along the Spurwink Island Path, part of the East Coast Trail between Aquaforte and Port Kirwan. Carved by the continuous wave and ice action of the North Atlantic, the arch began as a sea cave before its roof collapsed, creating the arch. The arch is one of the few in the province that has grass and small trees growing on its top, providing those who dare the chance to walk on top of it. Caution should be exercised due to the slippery conditions often experienced on the trail and the arch's high elevation.

Even without the walk on top, the arch is worth the hike. Located on the south side of Aquaforte harbour, the arch is hardly the only feature in the harbour. Hidden beaches, sea caves, and several sea stacks are also found along this stretch of coastline—though a boat or sea kayak is required for the best view.

⊕ **BERRY HEAD SEA ARCH: N 46.998406, W 52.900190**
The arch is located along the Spurwink Island Trail, part of the East Coast Trail. From the two trailheads in Aquaforte and Port Kirwan, a hike of approximately 9 kilometres or 8.2 kilometres, respectively, is required.

Pouch Cove
5
Bauline
Flatrock
Torbay
6
Bell Island
1
2
Portugal Cove
7
12
3
9
St. John's
8
Cape S
10
11
Conception Bay South
Paradise
4
Petty Harbour
Holyrood
Bay Bulls

Northeast Avalon

If you live outside the province, the idea of the northeast Avalon and, more specifically, St. John's, as a major urban centre may be amusing, but for those who grew up outside the region, St. John's might as well be Toronto. Conception Bay South, Paradise, Mount Pearl, and St. John's collectively contain almost the same population as the rest of the island combined.

Make no mistake, Paradise and Mount Pearl have their own histories and cultures to explore, but downtown St. John's is one of the province's most vibrant cultural and historic districts. The merchant buildings and historic commercial districts of Water Street and Duckworth Street offer some of the finest dining and accommodations in the province. And this excludes George Street, which claims the title of having the most bars and pubs per square kilometre in North America. Just a short distance away is Cape Spear, the most easterly point in North America and, to the north, are the smaller towns of Torbay, Pouch Cove, and Portugal Cove-St. Philip's. And just 20 minutes from the capital city is the Bell Island ferry. Located in the middle of Conception Bay, Bell Island once had thriving mines and, although the mines have closed, the spectacular geology and geographic formations along its coast are not to be missed.

St. John's is one of the oldest European cities in North America. Attracted by the protected harbour, seasonal and, later, permanent fishers built fishing sheds, flakes, and houses. The area developed into a merchant town before evolving into the hub of Newfoundland. Settlers also moved to the surrounding communities; the uninhabitable coastline meant that many were forced to build their fishing flakes, sheds, and houses along the cliffsides, signs of which are still seen today. In Mount Pearl, Paradise, and Kilbride, the first residents were farmers and loggers.

But as the city of St. John's continued to grow, it enveloped these places, creating a continuous urban landscape. The discovery of offshore oil in 1979 catalyzed growth and expansion, not only in the region but for the entire island.

St. John's, Mount Pearl, and Paradise can be explored using semi-reliable public transportation networks such as the local Metrobus system. But to travel among the close surrounding towns, a vehicle is required. Route 20 leads north to Torbay and Pouch Cove; Route 2, from downtown St. John's to Conception Bay South; and Routes 40 and 50, to Portugal Cove-St. Philip's, where vehicle ferry sails to Bell Island, just 20 minutes away.

1. Bell Island Mine

Bell Island, Conception Bay

Bell Island is a small island 5 kilometres offshore in Conception Bay with a big history in mining. During the mine's operation between 1895 and 1965, some 78,989,400 tons of iron ore were extracted and, at the time of its closure, the Bell Island mine was the longest continually operating mine in Canada.

Now with a population of around 2,000, the island's only town, Wabana, is a fraction of the size it was during its peak years. Previously home to 13,000 people, the island is littered with repurposed and abandoned buildings, empty fields where mining operations once took place, and large hills of waste rock and ore.

HISTORY

The first recognition of Bell Island's mineral potential was in 1578 when reports were sent to England regarding the possible iron occurrences on the island. Samples were sent to England in 1628 by John Guy's colony in Cupers Cove (modern-day Cupids), but it was not until the late 19th century that any major mining operations were undertaken. In 1892, mineral rights were purchased by Jabez H. Butler and, after consulting with the New Glasgow Coal, Iron, and Railroad Company (later named the Nova Scotia Steel and Coal Company), a deal was made to start a mine.

In the summer of 1895, mining operations began. The first mines dug on Bell Island exploited the shallow layer of iron above sea level. The ore bed on Bell Island gently dips to the northwest. Miners began extracting ore near the surface farther inland and followed the naturally dipping bed underground until

they pierced the cliffs on the northwest coast. These mines would be named Numbers 1 and 5.

As the ore was extracted, roughly 40 per cent was left in place to form pillars to support the roof, a method of mining known as the "room and pillar method." The general layout consists of a hatched pattern of tunnels running perpendicular and parallel to the coastline.

In 1899, the Whitney Company (later named the Dominion Steel Corporation) also began a mining operation on Bell Island after purchasing the rights to a deeper ore bed. With surface amounts depleting by 1905, the new company opened subsurface mines Numbers 2, 3, 4, and 6.

These "submarine" mines extended far out underneath Conception Bay. The mines were larger than the shallow-depth

mines and stretched approximately 5 kilometres out beneath the bay, with depths ranging from 60 metres to nearly 490 metres below sea level.

Sophisticated water pumping systems were installed to keep the mine from flooding due to seeping groundwater. The submarine mines also used the room and pillar method; however, due to greater depths and the weight of the ocean, 60 per cent of the ore was unmined to provide support.

Both shallow and submarine mines featured:

- Straight uniform tunnels measuring roughly 4 metres wide and 4 metres high.
- A main control shaft from which all others branched. This shaft provided the main entrance to the mine and was used to bring ore to the surface.

- A series of telephone lines that connected workers below ground to those above. In the mines today, pieces of insulators and cables that made up this system are still visible.
- Water pumping systems to prevent water build-up in areas below the groundwater table.
- A system of railway tracks and ore carts to transport the ore to the surface. Ore was transported along the branch tunnels to the main shaft, where it would be gradually lifted up the inverted slope to the surface via steam-powered engines.
- A system of iron pipes to transport air to operate the miner's compressed-air mining tools.

The mines operated successfully through the first half of the 20th century. When World War II began in 1939, the increased demand for steel and iron made Bell Island more important than ever. This importance was not ignored by Germany, and on September 5 and November 2, 1942, four ore ships were torpedoed and sunk by German U-boats. The attack sunk ore freighters SS *Saganaga*, SS *Lord Strathcona*, SS *PLM 27*, and SS *Rose Castle*, killing 70 merchant mariners. After the attack, a coastal defence battery was constructed near the modern-day ferry terminal.

The mines continued operating until 1949, when one of the shafts was shut down. Two more shafts were shut down in 1959 and 1963, and the final mine in 1966. At the time of its closure, the Bell Island mine was the longest continually operating mine in Canada. The main reason for the closure was that the Sydney steel mills in Nova Scotia, where the ore was primarily shipped, were unable to compete with foreign competition and they also shut down in 1966.

1916
DANGER
FALLING ROCK
KEEP OUT

ABOUT THE AREA

The mining operation on Bell Island covered a significant portion of the island. In the north, the town of Wabana was established and was the central location for the mining operations and where most people lived. Bell Island mining operations were largely confined to the northwest coast of the island, adjacent to the town, while shipping facilities were located on the southeast side, near the modern-day ferry terminal.

Today the area where the mines were once located remain barren and, with the exception of several new houses, consist mainly of grassy fields and empty lots. Winding throughout this barren landscape today are Bell Island's many trails, pathways, and dirt roads. Travelling along these by foot, bicycle, or recreational vehicle is the best way to explore the landscape, where pieces of equipment and lost buildings are abundant.

 ### NO. 2 MINE BELL ISLAND COMMUNITY MUSEUM:
N 47.646450, W 52.949212

The safest and most informative way to experience the mines and learn more about them is to visit the No. 2 Mine Museum. Here, you can safely enter No. 2 mine to glimpse what it was like to work in the mines. Inside are mine cart tracks, piping, and workers' shelter. After walking into the former mine for several hundred metres, the underground shafts disappear into a cloudy pool, marking the beginning of the flooded section.

Back above ground and adjacent to the mine is one of many tailings piles that contain rocks determined to have an insufficient level of ore and thus not worth transporting to market.

A short distance from the No. 2 mine is the entrance to the No. 4 mine. Now sealed shut, the concrete tunnel dips below ground, marking the start to a tunnel several kilometres long.

Shallow Mines

Along the northwest coast of the island, it is also possible to see the openings of the shallow mines first excavated. Best seen from a boat or sea kayak, the coastal cliffs are spotted with small openings, many of which have collapsed due to years of coastal waves pounding the rocks. Hiking to the area known as the Grebes Nest also allows a closer look at the mines and the sloping plateau that was created from years of mineral extraction. It is here, however, where you get the best sense of how dangerous

this area is, as collapsed openings, slippery coastal rocks, and the crumbling cliffside are reminders to keep a safe distance.

Big Cove

Located between two headlands, surrounded by vertical cliffs, Big Cove and the beach within were well known by locals as one of the best spots for catching capelin in the spring/summer of the year. But the steep, surrounding cliffs hiding the isolated beach made the cove impossible to reach. As many of the people living on Bell Island had experience with underground mining, residents found a solution: dig a tunnel through the headland. Today this tunnel located near the Grebes Nest is visible and can be traversed.

⊕ **GREBES NEST:** N 47.640864, W 52.978765

Fossils

The layered Ordovician shale and sandstone that provided Bell Island with its iron ore left many trace fossils of past organisms. These fossils are found along the island coast and typically resemble tubelike structures protruding out of the rocks. These fossils were formed by organisms burrowing into the ancient sea floor, where they lived nearly 450 million years ago. Nowhere is this better seen than in the Grebes Nest.

⌖ NO. 2 MINE BELL ISLAND COMMUNITY MUSEUM (CENTRAL BELL ISLAND): N 47.646450, W 52.949212

The ferry to Bell Island is located in Portugal Cove-St. Philip's, approximately 13 kilometres from St. John's. The ferry trip is only 20 minutes long, and inexpensive. The ferry makes regular daily trips and tickets can be purchased at the terminal. When you drive off the boat, follow the road into the town of Wabana.

2. Bell Island Battery
Bell Island

During World War II, the demand for iron and steel, critically important in the production of ships, vehicles, and weapons, escalated. Seemingly overnight, the Bell Island iron ore mines became one of the most important places in Newfoundland. The ore, shipped to steel mills in Sydney, Nova Scotia, was, as a result, vulnerable to attack by German U-boats. Recognizing this, the Canadian and British governments established one of Newfoundland's first military installations of the war on Bell Island. The installation was equipped to identify enemy ships, submarines, and aircraft and, if necessary, provide a counter or defensive attack.

The battery in the spring of 1940 consisted of two 4.7-inch quick-firing guns on concrete platforms overlooking the Dominion and Scotia loading piers (near the current ferry terminal). When it opened in the summer of 1940, the Canadian Army operated the site, until the Newfoundland militia took command after receiving proper training.

On September 4, 1942, German U-boat U-153 followed the ore ship *Evelyn B* into the Bell Island port. The following morning German Lieutenant Rolf Ruggeberg fired multiple torpedoes at the SS *Saganaga* and the SS *Lord Strathcona*, sinking both and taking 29 lives in the process. The Newfoundland militia stationed at the battery fired several shots at the U-boat but did not sight it. The attack shocked the people of Newfoundland, who had not contemplated an attack on a non-military ship in the protected bay. The sinking of the two ships and the battery's failed attempt to respond to the attack led to a larger military presence in the bay and improvements to the battery, including the installation of large searchlights, regular training, and stationed troops on a constant state of alert.

Even with these additional measures, just two months later the next set of attacks came when German U-boat U-518 entered Conception Bay. Under the command of Kapitan-Leutnant Friedrich Wissmann, the U-boat carefully entered the bay and on November 2, 1942, fired its first torpedo at the freighter *Flyingdale*, which was tied to the pier. The torpedo missed the ship and passed under its hull, exploding once it hit the pier. Next, the U-boat fired at the ore carrier SS *Rose Castle* and the French vessel *PLM 27*. Twenty-eight men were lost on the *Rose Castle* and another 12 on the *PLM 27*. Although a corvette warship and two small patrol boats quickly responded to the attacks, and

the battery provided oversight of the area, the U-boat escaped undetected.

When the war ended, so did the threat to the Bell Island ships. Decommissioned, the Bell Island battery was turned into a memorial to those who served in the war and to those who fought to keep Newfoundland's shores safe. Today, the battery and its two guns have been restored; the site also offers panoramic views of Conception Bay.

BELL ISLAND BATTERY: N 47.630455, W 52.927089
After departing the Bell Island ferry terminal, travel 1 kilometre and turn onto Memorial Street. Travel 700 metres and turn left onto the small street of Cemetery Hill. The battery is located at the bottom of the hill, approximately 400 metres away.

3. The Bell

Bell Island

Dotting Bell Island's distinctive steep, layered cliffs are dozens of sea caves and sea stacks. But none of them compares to the sea stack located on its southwestern side, known as "The Bell." Like its parent island, the sea stack's sides are composed of layered sedimentary rocks and on top is a vegetated, grassy field. Separating the sea stack from Bell Island is a 45-metre-wide channel that can be navigated by boat on a calm day at high tide. A short hike is required to get to The Bell. For your efforts you will be rewarded with views of Conception Bay and other sea stacks and isolated beaches.

⊕ **THE BELL:** N 47.607778, W 53.024537

On Bell Island, travel to the end of Lance Cove Road, which follows the southern side of the island, or to the end of Middleton Avenue, which follows the northern side. Turn onto Belle Road. The trailhead (N 47.599481, W 53.011770) is located at the end of this road. A 1.3-kilometre-long coastal trail brings you to the sea stack.

4. Kelligrews Abandoned Pool

Kelligrews, Conception Bay South

As the Kelligrews River travels to Conception Bay South, it briefly flows through a wide pool lined by concrete walls, and at its egress is a partly opened dam. The rectangular pool was once an outdoor pool operated by the town and a popular spot among locals to get away from the summer heat. Opened in the mid-1970s, it operated for 15 years. Its closure in the early 1990s resulted from

concerns over poor water quality due to an upstream landfill and also continued acts of vandalism at the pool.

 **KELLIGREWS ABANDONED POOL:** N 47.477555, W 53.012046

The trailhead (N 47.481088, W 53.016799) is located at the end of Gateway Drive near its intersection with Legion Road. Follow the dirt path down the hill, keeping right, to reach the outdoor pool.

5. NASA's Satellite Tracking Station
Pouch Cove

Newfoundland's contribution to space technology surprises many. But from 1960 to 1983, Newfoundland's strategic location at the northeastern tip of North America made it a critical location for tracking NASA satellites and spacecraft launched from the Kennedy Space Center in Cape Canaveral, Florida.

Built in 1960, it was one of 12 stations constructed as part of the Satellite Tracking and Data Acquisition Network (STADAN). During its operation, the station calculated trajectories, aiding in communicating and tracking spacecraft launched from the NASA facility. Its most notable use was tracking and communicating with the Apollo lunar missions throughout the 1960s and early 1970s. As the technology became obsolete in the 1970s, the complex was transferred to the Canadian government and used mainly for research in partnership with Memorial University. The station was shut down in 1983.

Today, with the exception of one administration building being used by the Lions Club, the site has been abandoned. Most of the foundations and support structures for the satellite dishes and radar are still visible.

TRACKING STATION: N 47.740926, W 52.720774

The site is located in the town of Pouch Cove, north of St. John's. Drive approximately 2.6 kilometres past Windgap Road, Flatrock, on Route 20 toward Pouch Cove and turn onto Satellite Road. The site is at the end of the road.

6. Red Cliff Radar Station
Logy Bay-Outer Cove-Middle Cove

Perched on the hills above the community of Logy Bay is a complex of roads, foundations, and odd-shaped buildings that once made up the Red Cliff Radar Station. This Cold War-era site was once a critical component of a network of radar stations known as the Pinetree Line. Designed to detect Soviet aircraft and missiles over the Atlantic Ocean and the Arctic, the complex still contains many intriguing places to explore, just minutes from the province's largest city.

HISTORY

During the Cold War, fear of attack by the Soviet Union led the United States Air Force (aided by the Royal Canadian Air Force) to construct a system of radar stations known as the Pinetree Line. These sites, all located approximately along the 50th line of latitude, stretched across the continent. In 1951, the hills behind Logy Bay, were chosen to host the most eastern site.

Construction began in 1951 on the radar system and a complex of buildings that would make the site completely self-sustaining: the operations building, barracks, a steam power plant, and other essential buildings. A secondary radar system and operations building were also builtt lower on the hillside near the site of a World War II lookout battery. The radar site, completed in 1953, was operated by American service members from the 108th AC&W Squadron who were later re-designated the 642nd Aircraft Control and Warning Squadron.

The radar site recorded aircraft speed, altitude, and direction

over the North Atlantic. If an aircraft was unable to be identified, the information was passed on to fighter jets located nearby at the Torbay Airport (now St. John's International Airport). The radar site also provided navigational assistance to friendly aircraft and search and rescue operations.

Although it was one of the most advanced sites of its time, rapidly advancing technology made it obsolete and, on October 1, 1961, it was closed. Many of the buildings were relocated to other military bases or demolished. Most of the concrete structures that made up the radar foundations, operations building, and power plant were left to deteriorate. The site's electrical systems and

radar equipment were transported to Harmon Air Force Base in Stephenville and reused or decommissioned.

ABOUT THE AREA

Throughout the forest and roads leading to the site, vehicles, oil drums, and pieces of equipment remain half-buried in the hillside. At the main site, the circular structure that once hosted the main radar dome is still standing and clearly visible. Nearby is the concrete operations building. Down the road are the site's facilities and power generation plant. The concrete buildings and water tank are slowly deteriorating; as of 2021, they remain standing

among the trees and tall grass. While the road to the site is gravel, about halfway up the hillside, a side road heading north is paved. At the end of this road is the secondary radar site and World War II battery. The concrete operations building continue to stand atop the mountain and closer to the edge of a nearby cliff is the concrete battery, buried in the hillside.

The Red Cliff Radar Station is the best-preserved Cold War-era radar site in the province. Red Cliff offers a unique chance to explore a site, built out of fear of entering another, devastating war, and designed to protect North America if required. The entire hillside is explorable, with many trails leading through the forest, including Cobbler's Path, part of the East Coast Trail.

RED CLIFF RADAR STATION: N 47.639723, W 52.666787

The site is located in Logy Bay-Outer Cove-Middle Cove. From Marine Drive, follow Red Cliff Road to the cul-de-sac at its end. Park along the side of the road. Hike the gravel road for approximately 750 metres to a fork. Follow the paved road on the left for approximately 400 metres to the secondary radar site and World War II battery; follow the road to the right for approximately 400 metres for the main radar site.

You can also reach the site by hiking Cobbler's Path, part of the East Coast Trail. Leave from the southern trailhead on Marine Drive (N 47.656043, W 52.673668) or the northern trailhead at the end of Doran's Lane (N 47.626108, W 52.669488). A hike of approximately 1.8 kilometres or 3 kilometres is required, respectively.

7. Central Swine Breeding Station

Portugal Cove-St. Philip's, Northeast Avalon

Commonly and improperly referred to as a slaughterhouse, this complex of abandoned buildings off Portugal Cove Road in St. John's was once a farm that raised and supplied pigs for commercial use around the province. Officially named the Central Swine Breeding Station, the 150-acre breeding farm was established in the 1960s.

In 1965, the Government of Newfoundland and Labrador set up a breeding program that provided assistance and subsidiaries to the commercial swine industry. The program supplied pathogen-free livestock to 16 commercial producers and was involved in testing new breeding techniques and methods of genetically modifying livestock.

The station operated for just over 25 years until 1993, when the Newfoundland and Labrador government decided it was no longer viable and cut the $800,000 annual government funding.

The site itself consisted of 10 swine sheds, an office and storage building, a large concrete manure storage tank, and other sheds and structures. Today, deteriorated structures, asbestos, poor air quality, and dangerous chemicals pose a major risk to visitors. Because of this and the continuous calls of action from local residents to demolish the site, the provincial government has constructed a chain-link fence around the area to deter possible trespassers, vandals, or curious explorers. If you venture to this site, experience it from a safe distance.

 **CENTRAL SWINE BREEDING STATION:** N 47.609725, W 52.801741

Travel approximately 4 kilometres past the St. John's International Airport on Portugal Cove Road (toward Portugal Cove) and turn onto Powers Road. The station is located on a small gravel road adjacent to the Tilt House Bakery.

8. Fort Amherst

St. John's Harbour

Beneath Fort Amherst Lighthouse in the St. John's Narrows is a concrete complex of buildings, staircases, and rooms. The complex, built to protect the city during the Second World War, is one of the last visible reminders of this turbulent time. Today, the area is best known for its views of the harbour and of the ocean, while the deteriorating remnants often go unnoticed.

HISTORY

The fortification of Fort Amherst began long before World War II. Its position at the entrance of the harbour has long made it a strategic location. The first fortifications were placed in the mid-18th century to protect fishers and their families using the harbour from, primarily, French invaders. This came in response to the 1762 attack on English-occupied St. John's when French forces from nearby Plaisance (later Placentia) captured the city and burned most of it to the ground. The city was recaptured by the English, under the leadership of Lieutenant-General William Amherst, for whom the fort is named. That battery was demolished in 1813 to make way for the construction of Newfoundland's first lighthouse, whose foundations can still be seen below the modern lighthouse. In the wake of World War II, Fort Amherst was fortified to protect the harbour, but never required for use.

World War II

The story of the fortifications visible today begins in November 1940 when the area was commissioned as a "Q" battery, also

AVALON SEA

known as an "examination battery," by the Royal Canadian Navy. Its troops stationed there were in charge of locating and tracking unidentified ships nearing the harbour. If a ship did not display identification or seemed suspicious, an examination boat intercepted it and checked its credentials. The battery's strict orders were to fire on any uncooperative ship.

In 1941, the increasing importance of St. John's as a rallying point for transatlantic shipping convoys required that the fort be more fortified. That fall, several buildings and a large, two-gun battery were built beneath the lighthouse. The 103rd

Coast Battery unit of the Royal Canadian Artillery operated two 7.3-metre-long, 120-millimetre, quick-firing guns which replaced the original 75-millimetre guns originally installed in the battery.

To house the 92 soldiers stationed at Fort Amherst, a large two-storey barracks and several support buildings were built to the west of the site, along the road to the battery. The soldiers oversaw the operation of the fort, including the operation and deployment of the anti-torpedo nets that stretched across the harbour, and the controlled underwater minefield placed outside the Narrows to protect against enemy U-boats.

March 3, 1941, U-boat Attack

The fort's defences were tested on the night of March 3, 1941, when German U-boat U-587 sneaked past the military defence battery at Cape Spear and Signal Hill and fired three torpedoes at the steamer *Terra Nova* as it approached the harbour. This was likely done to sink the steamer across the mouth of the harbour, known as the Narrows, and block ships from passing into the harbour and disrupting their military efforts. One torpedo was caught in the anti-torpedo nets stretched across the Narrows. The other two exploded on the cliffs below the fort, reportedly sending a spray of water high above the battery. Improvements in the harbour's protection followed, including new anti-torpedo nets and a controlled minefield that was placed off the harbour's entrance in June 1942.

In 1946, after the end of the war, the battery was decommissioned, and the following year the area was transferred to the Newfoundland government. In 1954, the original stone-built lighthouse was demolished to make way for the 6-metre-high wooden lighthouse and nearby housing residence located there today. Within one of the foggiest capitals in Canada, the lighthouse and foghorn continue to be used as important navigational aids to ships entering and leaving St. John's harbour.

ABOUT THE AREA

Fort Amherst is located on the south side of St. John's harbour. During the summer, it is a popular location from which to spot whales and icebergs as they pass the Narrows.

Seventy-five years of relentless exposure to the ocean has taken a toll on the concrete structure. Large pieces of concrete walls and stairs have collapsed from the main structure and fallen into the surf. And while it has eroded significantly, the main structure of the battery, including the gun emplacements and surrounding ammunition bunkers, are still relatively intact. The deterioration is severe enough that Parks Canada, which maintains the site, has prohibited access to the complex itself. The best vantage points today are along the North Head Trail, which winds around Signal Hill, as well as the current road to Fort Amherst, and at Fort Amherst itself.

SOUTHSIDE HILLS DAMS: N 47.560053, W 52.685170

The water supply for the battery came from a dam constructed on Soldier's Pond located on the Southside Hills. Soon after the dam was built, however, the water was deemed unfit for drinking, and while the dam was maintained for firefighting purposes, the endeavour was mostly abandoned. Seventy-five years later, the dam is responsible for one of the city's most popular swimming locations.

FORT AMHERST: N 47.563435, W 52.680434

From downtown St. John's, travel to the end of Southside Road (which turns into Fort Amherst Road). Pass the marina and park in the parking lot in the rock cut at the top of the hill. From the parking lot, a 600-metre-long walk along the paved roadway takes you to Fort Amherst.

9. Chain Rock

North Head Trail, St. John's

Chain Rock, on the north side of St. John's harbour, below the Queens Battery on Signal Hill, was one of the city's first defence fortifications. Built in the mid-18th century, it was an anchor point for a large chain that would be placed across the Narrows each night to prevent enemy ships from entering.

In 1941, Chain Rock was commissioned again by the Royal Canadian Navy to protect the Narrows: the anchor point for the anti-torpedo nets that spanned the harbour to protect it from German U-boats and torpedoes. During this time, the fortification was converted into a two-gun Anti-Motor-Torpedo-Boat battery to protect the minefield placed outside St. John's harbour. Two 75-millimetre guns were transferred from the Fort Amherst Battery in 1941 to Chain Rock. Two 150-centimetre-diameter searchlights aided in U-boat and aircraft detection.

Today, the area can be accessed at the lower entrance to the North Head Trail. Several concrete buildings remain and, close to the water, anchoring points protrude from the coastal rocks and foundations of the original fort.

CHAIN ROCK: N 47.567553, W 52.687329

Leaving from the bottom of Signal Hill Road, turn onto Battery Road and park next to the intersection with Cabot Avenue. Walk 220 metres and turn downhill onto Outer Battery Road. Continue to the North Head trailhead (N 47.567979, W 52.687871). The battery is 60 metres along the trail.

10. Bowring Park Cantilever Bridge
Bowring Park, St. John's

In the early 1950s, the Canadian National Railway began planning a pedestrian bridge across the railway tracks running through Bowring Park. At the time, Montreal architecture firm van Ginkel Associates was extending the park. When approached to construct the bridge, the firm acquired the help of UK structural engineering firm Ove Arup and Partners to design a modern and aesthetically pleasing bridge.

Sir Ove Arup, who helped design the Sydney Opera House, chose a cantilever bridge. The concrete bridge would rest on an off-centre support located on one side of the tracks and the weight of the lower side offset that of the upper side. As a result, the main span of the bridge is unsupported except at the lower end, where it attaches to the pier. If you look closely, you see that the bridge does not touch the abutment on the higher end.

The completed bridge was an engineering marvel and a symbol of the modern age. In 1966, Sir Ove Arup was awarded a Royal Gold Medal by the Royal Institute of British Architects and reportedly claimed the Sydney Opera House and the Bowring Park Bridge as his career highlights.

The bridge has recently undergone much-needed repairs.

CANTILEVER BRIDGE: N 47.526334, W 52.748311
From the lower Bowring Park parking lot (N 47.529409, W 52.744839), the bridge is approximately 500 metres away on a walking path that is now part of the Newfoundland T'Railway.

11. Brookfield Drive-In

Mount Pearl, Avalon Peninsula

Located off Tobin's Road in Mount Pearl are the remains of Newfoundland's last drive-in movie theatre. The theatre was opened in 1973 by US-based businessperson Chuck Baldwin. The theatre quickly became a popular spot, with hundreds of people gathering in their vehicles on movie nights.

It wasn't long before VCRs and home theatres rose in popularity, and the drive-in declined. It also struggled to compete with the region's infamous rain, drizzle, and fog, but it was not until the fall of 1992 when the final blow (literally) came.

In October 1992, a powerful wind and ice storm caused extensive damage to the theatre. *The Telegram* reported that "the screen's support posts were torn from their underground concrete anchor and parts of the screen were blown into the field behind the drive-in." Part of the screen even came close to landing on Pitts Memorial Drive, which could have injured those travelling on the busy road. Baldwin had planned to open the drive-in the following year, but decided against it.

After the drive-in's abrupt closure in 1992, the theatre and the land were abandoned. The boarded-up snack bar, projection booth, and speaker poles remained standing until October 3, 2003, when two pumper trucks were called to a bush fire in the vicinity of the old drive-in, only to find the snack bar and projection booth ablaze.

When the trucks arrived, they found the canteen located in the centre of the property on fire. The trucks were forced to stop 200 metres from the blaze due to obstructions that had been meant to

protect the site from vandals and curious trespassers. After a local excavator finally removed the barriers, the firefighters arrived at the smoldering remains of the canteen and projection building.

The theatre was a cultural icon to those living in the area. Like all drive-in theatres in the province, it faced many challenges and its closure was inevitable. Although the site has grown in with trees and shrubs, remnants of the theatre are still visible. The original ticket welcomes those who wander through the mostly empty field. The rubble of the canteen and projection house lies in the middle of the field, where the vague outline of parking

spots and roadways are marked by an occasional steel speaker post. These remnants serve as a slowly disappearing reminder of the Brookfield Drive-In and all drive-in theatres in the province.

⌖ BROOKFIELD DRIVE-IN: N 47.504946, W 52.780782

The drive-in was located off Brookfield Road in Mount Pearl, at the end of Tobin's Road on the north side of Pitts Memorial Drive. The theatre area is immediately adjacent to the road hidden in the overgrown field.

12. Military Batteries of the East Coast
Flatrock to Cape Spear

During the early years of World War II, Newfoundland was continuously militarized. The construction of Canadian, American, and British military bases meant that defending Newfoundland from German attack was critical to the war efforts. The waters outside St. John's harbour were a gathering place for transatlantic ship convoys that regularly transported troops, equipment, and aid to England. This vulnerability was recognized early, and in partnership with the Canadian military, the US Department of Defense selected sites for military lookouts and defensive batteries. In the early 1940s, numerous bunkers were constructed as defence bunkers and as lookout stations that could identify and report enemy U-boat sightings.

⊕ CAPE SPEAR BATTERY, CAPE SPEAR NATIONAL HISTORIC SITE: N 47.523707, W 52.621272

Famous as North America's most easterly point and for possessing Newfoundland's oldest lighthouse, for a short period during World War II Cape Spear was a critical defensive battery.

In November 1941, construction was completed on a large coastal defence battery which consisted of two 10-inch American guns, capable of being raised and lowered to hide from enemy ships. In addition to the gun emplacements, a network of underground rooms, tunnels, ammunition bunkers, and numerous searchlights aided in spotting enemy ships and aircraft.

The Cape Spear Battery may be the most accessible World War II remnant in Newfoundland today. It is located on the cliffs behind the Cape Spear National Historic Site. Accessible boardwalks and informative signs provide easy access to the site.

◎ BLACKHEAD "DUMMY" BATTERY, BLACKHEAD, ST. JOHN'S: N 47.531233, W 52.642842

Cape Spear is one of the province's most popular tourism destinations and any visitor will have seen the large World War II defensive battery built into the cliffside below the lighthouse. But what many people do not know is that high on a hill above the nearby town of Blackhead was a decoy or dummy battery. It had two purposes: to discourage attack by making the area look more

fortified than it was and to distract the enemy or draw their fire in the event of an attack.

The battery was constructed during World War II immediately after the battery at Cape Spear was built. Two fake guns believed to be telegraph poles were placed atop the hill and surrounded by a series of rock walls, which remain today.

The battery is located on the East Coast Trail between the town of Blackhead and Cape Spear. Hike approximately 1 kilometre east from the Blackhead trailhead or 1.5 kilometres west from the Cape Spear trailhead to the site.

RED CLIFF RADAR STATION BATTERY, LOGY BAY-OUTER COVE-MIDDLE COVE: N 47.646783, W 52.661445

Even before a radar station was placed on the hills above Logy Bay, Red Cliff was home to a lookout battery and bunker. The battery, constructed in 1941, operated between 1942 and 1945. Today the concrete battery is nestled high on the hillside overlooking the bay. The two underground rooms have been buried completely

but a small collapsed opening in the roof provides the curious with a glimpse of the inside.

Park at the end of Red Cliff Road (N 47.638371, W 52.670531). Hike approximately 750 metres on the dirt road, turn left onto a paved section of trail, and walk another 600 metres to the battery located near the cliff edge. The battery is located just off the Cobbler's Path section of the East Coast Trail.

 ROBIN HOOD BAY LOOKOUT BATTERY, ST. JOHN'S:

N 47.600405, W 52.655003

This one-room battery at the head of Robin Hood Bay near the current St. John's landfill was constructed in the early 1940s and, although its concrete has deteriorated considerably, it remains in place on the exposed hilltop.

The battery is located on the Sugarloaf Trail approximately 3.3 kilometres from the trailhead at Quidi Vidi and 5.5 kilometres from the trailhead at the Ocean Sciences Centre in Logy Bay.

 FLATROCK LOOKOUT BATTERY, FLATROCK:

N 47.702326, W 52.698438

This battery was constructed on the rocky peninsula known as the Beamer in the town of Flatrock. Operated between 1942 and 1945, this small concrete bunker, another reminder of the effects of the war on Newfoundland, continues to watch over the waters south of the town.

The battery is on the Father Troy Trail. Park at the wharf on the southside of Flatrock (N 47.700707, W 52.702255) and hike approximately 350 metres to the southeast side of the Beamer to the battery on the edge of the hillside.

Exploring Further

A Research Guide to Newfoundland and Labrador

Having spent years searching for and learning the whereabouts and history of Newfoundland's hidden places, I have found many useful research sources that may be helpful to you too. I believe these are the best resources for learning about Newfoundland's history and planning your next adventure.

GENERAL HISTORY & RESEARCH

Encyclopedia of Newfoundland and Labrador

It was probably one of the least controversial things done by Joey Smallwood's government: Newfoundland and Labrador is the only province with its own encyclopedia set. The comprehensive contents contain a general description and/or history of all things related to the province. This five-volume encyclopedia is found in most libraries but can also be viewed on the Centre for Newfoundland Studies (CNS) online database.

Centre for Newfoundland Studies Collections

Founded in 1965 by Memorial University, the CNS collects written material related to Newfoundland and Labrador. Anything that cannot be found on their online database (collections.mun.ca) likely exists within the thousands of resources and collections at their centre in the Queen Elizabeth II Library in St. John's.

Newfoundland and Labrador Heritage Website

Aimed toward students and the public, this online collection of articles and photographs gives a brief overview of topics related to the province's geography, history, and culture. Visit www.heritage.nf.ca.

MAPS & AERIAL PHOTOGRAPHY

Google Earth

This online application is one of the most accessible programs for viewing satellite imagery and travel planning: www.google.com/earth/.

Department of Fisheries, Forestry, and Agriculture

The provincial government has numerous resources for mapping and satellite imagery. The best collection is the GIS and Mapping Division's website: gis-and-mapping-gnl.hub.arcgis.com.

GEOLOGY & MINING HISTORY

Department of Natural Resources' Geoscience Atlas

Belonging to the province's Geological Survey Division, this interactive atlas educates about and promotes potential mining operations. The atlas contains all known information in the province on mineral occurrences, mining history, geologic information, and more: www.geoatlas.gov.nl.ca.

Once upon a Mine: Story of Pre-Confederation Mines on the Island of Newfoundland

Written by Wendy Martin, this guidebook is the best single source for information about mining and mineral exploration on the island. Thanks to a partnership with the Newfoundland and Labrador Heritage Website, the guide has been transformed into an online interactive book: www.heritage.nf.ca/articles/ environment/once-upon-a-mine.pdf.

SHIPWRECKS & PLANE CRASHES

The Plane Crash Girl: Lisa Daly's Blog

Aviation archeologist Lisa Daly has documented, preserved, and educated people on Newfoundland's aviation history and, more specifically, on the numerous aircraft crash sites around the province. Her work has been published widely; the best way to follow her and the places she has visited is her website: www. planecrashgirl.ca.

Shipwreck Preservation Society

Although their website lacks content directly relating to shipwrecks, the Shipwreck Preservation Society is a fantastic organization set at preserving the island's shipwrecks through documentation, education, and advocacy. See their Facebook page or website at http://www.shipwrecksnl.ca.

NOTABLE WEBSITES, BLOGS, & TRAVEL-RELATED INFORMATION

Anglo-Newfoundland Development Company Historical Website and Facebook Page

This collection of articles, stories, pictures, and research on Central Newfoundland relates to the logging and forestry history of the region. It highlights how the industry has changed the landscape and the people that live in the area. This database is an example of what it means to successfully document and promote the culture and heritage of an area: anglonewfoundlanddevelopmentcompany.wordpress.com.

Community History Facebook Groups/Pages

Many public Facebook groups/pages have been started to share pictures, stories, and family trees related to particular communities or regions. Particularly helpful in writing this book were Historic Corner Brook; Twillingate and the Isles History; Old St. John's; Old Gravel Roads and Highways in Newfoundland. If your community does not have a group, consider starting one!

Index of Places

Photo Credits

Unless otherwise noted, all photographs were taken by Scott Osmond.

Thank you to the following photographers for contributing their work:

- Michaela Barnes (pages 87, 88, 93);
- Lindsay Batt (pages 65, 208, 243, 363);
- Isaac Bauman (page 402);
- Anthony Randell (page 90);
- Bev and Tom McIsaac (pages 20-1, 50, 100, 276, 277, 339, 451, 460);
- Sheridan Moores (414); and
- Whymarrh Whitby (pages 222-3, 224).

Acknowledgements

A huge thanks to all my family and friends who supported me through this endeavour, and especially to all those who joined me or, more importantly, showed me the way to many of the sites I describe. I must particularly thank my partner Lindsay Batt, who joined me for almost all the adventures in this book and whose motivation and desire for adventure made this book possible. A special thanks to the parent figures in my life: Tanya and Greg Osmond; Bev and Tom McIsaac, Mary Batt and Derrick Baldwin, and my grandmother Blanche Osmond. Each one supported and encouraged me over the last several years.

For helping me experience many of the places in this book, I want to thank: my good friend, Anthony Randell, who has joined me on countless adventures; Kim, Mike, Jordan, Allison and Eleanor Badcock who, on multiple occasions, provided amazing hospitality and were fantastic tour guides to some of the most amazing places on the Great Northern Peninsula; and Roy and Ben Osmond for taking me to places I could not have reached on my own, along with the support of Susan and Allison Osmond. An extra thank you to everyone who helped search for photos and provided me with information on the current condition of the sites in this book throughout the last year.

I want to send a special thank you to all the people who have followed, contributed, and supported HiddenNewfoundland.ca over the last seven incredible years and last, but certainly not least, to the hard work of my editor Stephanie Porter, copy editor

Iona Bulgin, designer Tanya Montini, publisher Gavin Will, and the entire Boulder Books team which helped make this book possible.

In a book filled with places to go, it is important to remember that it is not the place that makes the adventure, but the people who join you on the journey there.

Nikon
Nikon
EXPLORE NEWFOUNDLAND
Nikon

About the Author

Scott Osmond (he/him) is an adventurer at heart. Born and raised in Corner Brook, Newfoundland and Labrador, he completed a Bachelor of Civil Engineering and a Bachelor of Science in Geography at Memorial University of Newfoundland and Labrador in St. John's. In 2014, he established the website HiddenNewfoundland.ca to share the province's hidden places and lost stories. He is passionate about storytelling, heritage preservation, geography, and travelling. In between researching, writing, and planning his next adventure, he can be found kayaking, cycling, hiking, or simply enjoying a beer at a local brewery.